THE
NIGHT
HOUSE

*Folklore, Fairy Tales, Rites, and
Magick for the Wise and Wild*

Danielle Dulsky

New World Library
Novato, California

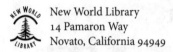

New World Library
14 Pamaron Way
Novato, California 94949

The material in this book is intended for education. It is not meant to take the place of diagnosis and treatment by a qualified medical practitioner or therapist. No expressed or implied guarantee of the effects of the use of the recommendations can be given nor liability taken. Names and identifying characteristics have been changed to protect privacy.

Text design by Tona Pearce Myers

Library of Congress Cataloging-in-Publication data is available.

First printing, March 2025
ISBN 978-1-60868-979-8
Ebook ISBN 978-1-60868-980-4

10   9   8   7   6   5   4   3   2   1

New World Library is committed to protecting our natural environment. This book is made of material from well-managed FSC®-certified forests and other controlled sources.

Printed in Canada

To Grammy Myrtle and all unruly women

Contents

Introduction

---✦---

Between a Once-Upon-a-Time
and an Ever-After

Come, my wise friend. Our traveling bundle is packed. The haunted road awaits, and the night birds are singing our song. Walk with me while the sun sets on our tamer ways. Raise your hood to the wind, whisper a heathen prayer of protection, and call the ancestral spirits closer. Our time in the day house has ended. The new story begins now.

While we walk, while the day takes its last breath, let me tell you of the wildest place I know. Deep in these woodlands stands a stone-and-bone house, a hidden place where the old tales live and breathe, a lost house where a sharp-tongued hag stirs her cookpot and waits for us, her story-hungry children. At the threshold of her Night House, we'll leave our civilized selves behind; she wouldn't have us any other way. Wearing our creaturely skins, we'll enter this forbidden place. We'll sip from her older-than-ancient brew, and we'll find a midnight home here.

Do you remember?

You've been to the Night House before. Only here, only when the shadows we cast stretch long, reaching back through the realms of deep time, are we reminded of a timely truth: The old ways of our ancestors are not lost. Hidden in the shadows of forest huts, tucked under the floorboards until the hunters have gone, a medicine bundle waits to be found. Our foremothers wrapped their secrets in bone and hair, blessed them with the wept and spat waters of their bodies, and hid their wilder ways between a once-upon-a-time and an ever-after.

If we look, we see the old stories are small books of magick. A fairy tale is a witch's grimoire disguised as a princess's dream, a *fate story* where the beauty and the beast are one and the same. As children we recognized those wonder stories as more than dead words on a page or cartoon faces on a screen. These stories had a heartbeat. They breathed for us and sang through us, shapeshifting every time we heard them, and we dwelled inside their secret passageways, bone castles, and woodlands of silver and gold. Transmitted through the hungry ears of wild innocents, these stories lived as they were meant to live, as folk teachings, original witchcraft lessons, medicine chests, and mirrors to our most radical intelligence.

If we dare return to these tales, we just might discover a forgotten piece of ourselves, a bit of the wolf's wisdom or the lyrics to the bone's song we remember only in our dreams. In this book, in our Night House, we hear the old stories as if for the first time. We meet them well, and we take our lessons from the dark, from the story-keeper who casts glamour spells with her tongue.

Return to the Night House

Somewhere, right now, a wild child listens to an old story for the first time. They imagine the grandmother-wolf's teeth and the Red Hood, the braided hair and the winged woman. Their untamed psyches conjure vivid images of seal-wives, talking foxes, and warrior maidens. For a time, they become the witch in the woods, the sleeping beauty, and the shadow on the road. Between the walls of a once-upon-a-time and an ever-after, they dwell inside this story. It is their healing house, their night school, the place where all possibilities exist at once.

If the tale has been kept well, if the sharpest shadows have been left intact, the story will surely sting the babe into a new and vital aliveness. In the space between the once and the after, that child is given vital tools for tending their transformation, for protecting their innocence and grieving well, for navigating the haunted road of a modern life. In the healing house of story, darkness is always welcome. The monsters sit at the same hearth as the bright-eyed innocents, and fear and hope are equally honored guests. While the child might receive a medicinal dose of wisdom from the fairy tale, these stories are hardly children's tales. Fairy tales were never intended only for children to hear and hold. These tales belong to us, the wild-hearted ones who know a thing or two about magick. The old stories are alive and full of spirits. An old story is immortal, a shapeshifter that swallows the many poisons of a time and spits back the exact medicine we need to heal. There are the stories that refuse death, that will live on a teller's tongue forever.

Though these stories have been given the stamp of approval by even the most puritanical caregivers over the years, though their vicious endings have been coated in pink icing and fed to the masses, the seeds of the deep and wicked wisdom remain. The shadow in every story still lives. The beast cannot be killed, and these are the days when we need those old stories most, when we must remember the tools we were given as wild-eyed children. In this volatile age of climate collapse, artificial intelligence, and broad sociopolitical turmoil, we are called to be tale-tenders. We are called to embrace and embody the wisdom of the dark.

Now more than ever, we must return to the Night House.

To Wreck the Ordinary, to Disturb the Familiar

A rebel loves a good trick. Our inner wild one is fed by those stories where the ordinary is wrecked by enchantment. The rebel archetype is the destroyer, the force that tramples expectation to bits and, for better or worse, the rebel always slow-dances with the trickster, the very essence of unpredictability that makes manifest the impossible. The rebel kills what must die so that the next possibility might live, and the trickster disturbs our best-laid plans.

Archetypes are containers of energy, living rivers of meaning that infuse and animate our heroes, villains, and those seemingly innocuous fringe characters who give shape to story. We live in story. We dream in story. We witness the whole of a life cycle in a single tale, from the birth of the exposition to the final death at the lysis, and we know in our marrow that a fairy tale holds far more power than its more recent labels and treatment connote.

A fairy tale, in itself, is a sort of trickster. The precise origins and nature of many fairy tales are impossible to define due to the oral tradition in which these stories were born. Some say these stories were born in someone's dream. Others say they were teaching tales rooted in religion, originally intended to keep us *good*. One truth is certain: The fairy tale cannot be caught, caged, and examined. Like a dancing sprite, it will suddenly appear at the dark crossroads, tell you a riddle, then disappear forever. What distinguishes a fairy tale, also known as a wonder story, from other folk tales is the element of magick. A fairy tale must, at least just once, defy the rational.

The supernatural always has a home in a fairy tale, and many metaphysical forces accepted and wielded in modern-day witchcraft and neo-pagan traditions are visible in these old stories. The importance of magickal discipline, the witch's perseverance, and maintaining a regular spiritual practice in the midst of adversity are all apparent in fairy tales, where the third time is, indeed, always the charm. The initiatory experience of the witch and the wise woman is made visible through fairy-tale journeys thick with underground forests and encounters with the cannibalistic hag. Through these stories, we learn to accept otherworldly truths, we meet our fears, and we rebel against logic.

If we see a fairy tale through the eyes of the rebel, we see the potent medicine such stories have to offer our world. As many unsustainable systems begin to fracture, our inner destroyer demands the timely death of the static and the immutable. Patriarchal structures thrive on *that's just the way it is*, but right now a little girl is reading about the old witch in the woods for the first time, and she understands the power of hidden wisdom, she knows that what she was told was *not real* in fact gives shape to her world, and she is imagining a future far stranger than the ordinary reality she is told to see.

The Hag's Secret

The trickster understands that nothing is as it seems. On the surface, a fairy tale is the innocent's bedtime story, a time-tested bridge between the waking world and the dreamworld. A fairy tale is a store-bought, prepackaged cake, or so it might appear, but if we scrape off that perfectly piped frosting, we find a bloody and beating heart beneath. We find the soft and rotten edges of shadow and the stink of feminine initiation. We find what we least anticipate, and our inner trickster laughs at the absurdity of our expectations.

These small stories historically lived on the woman's tongue, left locked outside the elite, male-dominated, scholarly fields of study. In *Shadow and Evil in Fairy Tales*, Marie-Louise von Franz, a close colleague of Carl Jung, wrote that "until about the seventeenth century, fairy tales were not reserved for children, but were told among grownups in the lower layers of the population — woodcutters and peasants and women while spinning amused themselves with fairy tales." These wonder stories were kept and transmitted primarily by women, spun slowly in the weaving rooms and the midwiferies. Nothing worthy of examination could be heard while the rocking chair squeaked, the contractions rocked the birthing bed, or the cookpot bubbled...or so they thought. Such stories were children's tales and nothing more, plots to be imagined by the psyches of innocents or used to pass the time while the seamstresses worked, stories that would be forgotten by the mature, rational mind, our happily-ever-after desires replaced by palatable ambitions and the witch's hut left to rot on the fringes of our more socially acceptable choices.

We were tasked to leave the fairy tale behind, to let it gather dust for a time alongside our dolls and play kitchens before we cast it out to the roadside. Worse, we were told the fairy tale was a prison, built to keep our world small and women caged in the archetypal boxes of princess, fragile mother, and fearsome sorcerer; yet, in those long-stretching midnight rituals of unexpected communion with the wild unseen, with a hidden intelligence that exists both beyond us and within us, we have a full-spirited understanding of a key truth the old fairy tellers knew well: Every fairy tale holds a piece of the old magick.

There are stories that can make or break a life, that can save or destroy an entire world, but not these stories, they said. These stories were just children's tales, after all; short and seemingly benign tales could hardly be a threat to the patriarchal powers that be. Few fairy tales house an empowered woman who survives or a mother who wins, and even fewer hold a formidable female as the main character. For these reasons, fairy tales were safe from the witch-hunter's noose. *Keep sharing these stories, Grannie, and let the little girls dream only of their royal knights, never mind the seduction of the wicked one's candy house or the woodland mist-spirits. Surely, it is the shining prince they want and not the shapeshifting, uncivilized beast. Surely, in the end, these stories will tame their wilder ways and keep them from venturing too far into the lawless borderlands.*

Even so, our inner rebel knows full well what a fairy tale really is. A fairy tale is a box of shadows. A fairy tale is a fiery witch's brew masked by a sweet but thin coating. The foremothers locked their spells, rituals, and rites inside these stories just for us. They let the fox-woman walk in the shadow of the good wife so she wouldn't be seen. They let the spell go wrong and the wolf come for the bad girl who dared to disobey, but the secrets are there if we look, laid bare for the curious eye and waiting for new story-keepers to come.

What if a hidden hand has been at work all along, leaving the foremothers to transmit, even unwittingly, the old earth-based mysteries? What if, in these dire times, something as seemingly pure as a fairy tale holds the very medicine we need to heal ourselves, our kin, and the world? What would happen if we dared speak these old stories aloud and let them live, let them teach us something new about what it means to be a wild woman, a good king, a witch, or a shapeshifter? What would happen if we re-membered these stories, reordering and revisioning them to be the very medicine our modern wounds require? Who might we become if we journeyed onto the otherworldly road, where we might meet the tricksters, the banshees, and the talking ravens, letting these monsters show us the way to the Night House, to the place we once knew and now must go again, as if for the first time?

A Curious Course in Mysteries

A story is a haunted house full of hidden doors, towering libraries, and underground apothecaries. The ways of the witch, the secrets kept hidden away in our books of shadows and cabinet altars, are visible in a story; we need only look deeper than we were told to look. Glamour spells and powerful charms reside in the story of Cinderella, the Girl from the Ashes. Lessons about ancestral healing and the shadows of the foremothers abound in the tale of Little Red Riding Hood, and the many stories of shapeshifting women and their wild skins have much to teach us about personal alchemy and transformation. Versions of "Beauty and the Beast," these *animal bridegroom* stories, beg us to wed our inner uncivilized one in a lifelong ceremony of liberation, and "Sleeping Beauty" holds the very key to the inner wise one's awakening.

None of these stories was ever solely about naive princesses and their enchantments. When we were told these tales as children, we heard echoes of the truly forbidden. The illustrations were pastel and glitter, but we saw the bones behind the gloss. We saw the invitation to name our own darkness in the villain's eyes. We pricked our finger on the rose behind the glass, sucked it dry, and tasted blood on our tongues. In our hearts, we knew these were night stories. These were tales to be told in the dark, and we would keep them close as we grew older, until the time came to unlock the old magick and name it truth.

In this book you will find invitations to wander the thin places, those 'twixt and 'tween wonderlands where the devils are always close. These are the haunts of the shapeshifters and wicked stepmothers, the mossy weeping stones and bone castles where mysteries, myth, rites, and rituals are made visible through familiar fairy tales. The invitation is to cross the threshold between the seen and the unseen, to honor the legacy of the forebears who tucked a spell inside a story just for us.

You are welcome to approach this work linearly, as a curious course in fairy tale mysteries you might live out loud, walking the night trail between the ordinary and the supernatural. Each chapter is a door to an otherworldly realm, a place at once familiar and strange, known and yet deeply buried in our secret psychic tunnels. Alternatively, you might hold this book as an oracle from time, scrying your future in the chapter that calls to you, in the divinatory rites of the Red Hood or the treacherous shadow work of the bone cellar.

The Rites of the Wild Skins,
Bone Cellars, and Spirit Towers

A rite is a ritual. If we mine the original meaning of the word, we come to understand that to enact a rite means "to observe carefully." For each of the thirteen rooms in the Night House, you will find the medicine of story and three rites for animating and amplifying the wisdom contained within the tale, for carefully observing and meaningfully encountering the deeply buried energies housed in the tale. These rites increase the medicine's potency, and they will not all be for you at all times. Trust that you will know which rites are yours and which ones should be left outside your experience for now.

Some stories will demand more time with you than others. Some rooms in the Night House will seem locked until you recover a bleeding key from your psychic shadows. Other rooms will swallow you whole and keep you there for a time. Some rooms will feel so familiar, so strangely safe, it will seem as if part of you has lived inside them your entire life.

The first four rooms of the Night House are the hidden rooms of the wild skins, dark places where the fires burn low in the hearth and the creaturely pelt hangs on the wall. Here you become part bird-woman, with feathers in your hair. You eat the foul flower and carry medicine to the grandmothers in your handwoven basket.

The bone cellar lies beneath the shapeshifter's lair, and here we strip ourselves bare. We encounter death, we leave gifts in the hollow of an oak for the Blackbird Boy, and we grieve the good mother as she takes her last breath. The shadows are sharpest here in these bloody chambers, but we learn much about the wounds of the world and our role as disruptor, radical healer, and tale-tender. Here we trouble our notions about who we are, and we disturb our palatable desires.

Finally, we ascend to the spirit tower, where dreams are more real than our waking life, where we sleep the sleep of initiation and remember why we were born to this time and place. We encounter our unique soul's truth here, our hallowed daemon, our inner guardian, and we hand-build our own house before the sun rises.

I invite you to imagine these stories as living containers of energy, breathing houses full of otherworldly meaning. In these stories, all characters, all images, are you. The lost child, the bold wanderer, and the blue-bearded shadow are all aspects of your own wild psyche. Keeping a journal close, move through the prompts, practices, and rites that speak to you, and remember that fairy tales were never merely children's stories. Allow the tales to mirror not only your personal myth but also the world story, who and where we are as a people, the ever-after we might collectively be moving toward so we might birth together our next once-upon-a-time.

Storytelling Is the Witch's Work

As you read this book, as you journey to and through the Night House, consider the hidden pieces of your own magick that are locked inside these old stories. What if they were stitched up in the hem of a nameless grandmother's apron just for you, to be unraveled right now, right here? The witch's ecological position in time and space is never an accident. We are always where and when we are meant to be, and the stories given to you as a child hold the very shadows you are meant to claim and name. The grandmother who rocks a babe on her lap and shares the story of "Beauty and the Beast" is doing more than telling a story; she is transmitting the old magick and gifting ancient wisdoms about wildness, initiation, and becoming whole.

My prayer is that you shake the pearls of sugar from these tales, remembering that a wonder story is, in the end, a book of shadows, a fate story, a small grimoire where mystery teachings were kept safe from the hunter-king's eyes. Many of the more famous male story collectors gathered their stories almost exclusively from women, after all, and storytelling has always been the witch's work. Allow each story to be a spell that disturbs time and invites a desired change. Give yourself permission to glean from stories personal understandings that are not outlined in these pages. Bid these stories to heal, protect, and change you, illuminating what you must see and who you must be.

Move through this curious course in mysteries as you would a haunted forest, with great care and night vision. Gather the golden eggs, and give aid to the creatures in need. Consider that fairy-tale wisdom is the very salve our ailing world needs right now, as we continue a human underworld journey through the terrors of a modern Bluebeard's castle and soften to the possibility that there are tales you are meant to keep and carry, harboring the deep wisdom safely tucked between the once-upon-a-time and the ever-after until the time is right to let it spill from your teller's tongue.

Into the dark we go.

Part I

Hidden Rooms
and Wild Skins

Chapter 1

The Red Hood

*In a well-honed crone, we may feel the transparency of her body that
is open to another reality. Being with her, we feel the presence of a
timeless, spaceless world. We begin to see everything from two sides —
the side that is totally in life and the side that is already dwelling in
disembodied soul.... She knows how tough and how gentle
we have to be to enter into this life and to leave it.*

MARION WOODMAN AND ELINOR DICKSON, *Dancing in the Flames*

We are made in the dark forests of initiation. Time and time
again, we leave who we used to be behind in the day house
while our emergent self takes to the woods. Here we face the midnight
terrors alone. Our breadcrumbs feed the birds, and we are lost again as
if for the first time in the lightlessness of uncertainty. The wolves howl,
and the witch within us wakes once more.

The initiatory wildland is an image common in fairy tales from
around the world. The haunted place where nothing is as it appears is
part of our shared human language, showing us the necessity of facing
death in our younger years, of having all we know stripped away in
order to become who we must now be. When we go into a dark woodland, we are animating an integral fairy-tale experience. We remember the old rites of passage because, in the end, we could never forget

them; they have been with us far longer than we have been without them. The oak trees groan, the night birds call, and we are not without fear, nor should we be.

Here we raise our red hoods and begin the journey along the otherworldly road. We can't help but break the rules we were given, and we know the hungry beast is always close. Even so, we leave the map for the daylit hours and step boldly into the dark unknown. Our grandmothers call to us, and we have no choice but to carry the medicine through the place of monsters. We have no choice but to slice open the wolf's belly and liberate not only ourselves but our forebears from the bowels of the beast.

Invitations for Tale-Tending: Initiation in the Haunted Woodland

As you enter this first room in the Night House, know that a threshold has been crossed. You hear the howl, see the bright-red cloak hanging from the wall, and understand full well that something wild is afoot. As you begin this journey, have faith in the intelligence of the story, knowing it will show you what you are meant to see. Let the story do its work on you, and remember these tales are oracles, yes, but they are showing you only what your deeper self already knows. Imagine this story was tucked away under a nameless grandmother's floorboards just for you, just for right now. Imagine this moment has been scripted, that it is no accident you are reading it at this moment, during this particular chapter in your story.

Stay attuned to the themes of initiation and lineage, shadow and ancestral healing. Remember that you are not only the innocent gathering flowers in the woods; you are also the ailing grandmother, the skilled hunter, and the wolf himself. This story has a spirit, after all, and that spirit has been transmitted in many forms through many generations. Notice the images in the tale that mark you, that feel especially vivid and true. Tend the spirit of this story, befriend the wolf, and you will understand the first piece of wisdom whispered in the Night House: You are healing the wounds of your grandmothers just by breathing.

*You are healing the wounds of your
grandmothers just by breathing.*

As evident in our guiding story, where the initiatory woodland is our timely teacher, the wild forest is where the great work gets done, where we face death and, in so doing, make the impossible possible. Here we become the maiden seeking the hag's hidden den. We face the monster, and we enact the rites of the haunted woodland.

Before our story begins, consider the image of the haunted woodland. How do you envision this underworld forest? What colors are there? What creatures wait for you? What time of day does it seem to be? What season? We all see this mythic, initiatory place differently.

Write a brief description of how you imagine this hallowed land. Use all your senses. What sounds do you hear? What does the wind smell like, and what tastes are on your tongue? Most importantly, how do you feel here?

Last, if this place could speak to you, what would its greatest lesson be? Name this message; it might be just a single word, or it may be longer, but ask yourself, What does this haunted woodland have to teach me right now, in this moment? Write this down, your message from the haunted woodland.

Story Altar: Gifts of the Red-Hooded One

As you begin to work with this story, build the tale a place to live. Like a spell, this is a symbolic action that invites the Otherworld to participate in your experience, to weave this story with you. Begin by speaking a spontaneous prayer to your ancestors, especially the long-gone-still-here ones whose names we may never know. Spread a red cloth, light a lone candle, and in a basket or another vessel, include symbols of your unique gifts, your strange and not-so-strange skills and talents, the treasures you acquired in this life and those you seemingly arrived with.

These may not be traits you would include on a traditional résumé, skills and talents that would be admired by the overculture. Perhaps you are able to see beauty in places where others see only rot. Perhaps you can bake a loaf of flavorful bread or brew a cup of medicinal tea like no other. Maybe you can build a mean fire, lead spontaneous rituals, or hold others in their grief. Take some time, and consider these treasures the tools of your inner warrior, the part of you who has come to this world prepared for the many battles that will surely come. Consider these gifts the stuff of destiny, orienting you toward your truest, most sacred work.

The Red Hood

Once in a time that was remembered, forgotten, and now is remembered again, there lived a dangerously curious little girl. She woke at dawn hungry for mystery, full of questions, and with wild eyes that saw everything as if for the first time. A rebellious child she was, and her mother and grandmother worried for her safety.

With each passing year, the girl was given more and more rules to live by. *Don't go outside after dark*, she was told. *Tell no one your name. By day, stick to the road and, when in doubt, run.*

On her seventh birthday, her grandmother stitched her a hood of bright red, the color of magick, sacrifice, and blood. The hood was meant to protect her, and the girl wore her red hood every day and every night. Over the years, she became known as Red Hood, and her first name was forgotten.

Around the time of Red Hood's first bleed, her grandmother fell quite ill. On a late-summer morning, she woke to find her mother preparing a basket full of bread, wine, and carefully foraged medicines.

"You are to take this to your grandmother, Red Hood," her mother said. "Stay on the road, speak to no one, and go as quickly as you can."

Red Hood, worried for her beloved grandmother, nodded, took the basket from her mother's hands, and hastened to the road. Never before had she been allowed to go to her grandmother's house all on her own. The way was haunted and hidden, yet she knew it well, and by noonday she was nearly there.

Proud of her timing, she slowed her pace. The late-summer sun was casting golden beams through the trees, the crows were cackling in her direction, and the wildflowers were in full bloom upon their forest beds of moss and pine needles. Suddenly, the basket felt quite heavy, and she decided to rest at the edge of the road.

Only then did she see the wolf.

"Oh, my dear child. What a lovely red hood you have!" The gray beast stepped out from behind a wide-trunked elm tree, white fangs gleaming, but Red Hood did not know to be afraid.

"Thank you," she replied. "My grandmother made it for me."

"How nice," the wolf crooned. "And where are you off to all alone?"

"I'm taking medicine to my grandmother. She's ill and too weak to leave her house," answered Red Hood.

"Oh, that's terrible news, my dear. Just terrible. May I ask, where does your grandmother live?" The wolf crept closer, head bowed, eyes fixed on Red Hood.

"Not far from here. Her house is where the oaks and the hazel grow together."

The wolf clicked his tongue. "Ah, I know it. Yes."

She could see the full size of him now, and her heartbeat quickened.

The wolf went quiet, pensive and plotting, and Red Hood thought she better be on her way.

"Wait," the wolf said as she stood, moving to block the road. "Do you see those pink flowers growing just there? A tea brewed from them will heal just about any ailment. Why don't you go and gather some? It won't take long."

"I…I better not. Good day to you." Red Hood curtsied and tried to move around the massive creature.

"Oh, but don't you want your grandmother to get well?"

Red Hood swallowed. She did, of course, want her grandmother to be well and whole.

"What's a few more minutes? Go on. Gather some of those flowers. She'll be healed by morning, I promise."

Red Hood pursed her lips, sighed, and agreed. "All right. I do want her to get better as quickly as she can."

The wolf smiled a great, sharp grin.

"That's a good girl. Well, I must be going. I hope your grandmother heals swiftly, and it was lovely to meet you."

With that the wolf was gone, running off into the shadows, and Red Hood left the road to gather the flowers. Lost in her work she quickly became, trying to pick only the brightest of the flowers, having to venture farther and farther into the forest, and before she knew it, hours had passed and it was nearly dark.

"Oh no!" Red Hood saw the sky turning amber behind the bony trees, and she ran back to the road, thinking of all her mother's rules she had broken that day.

Breathless, she made it to her grandmother's house before the moon rose. The door was wide open.

"Grandmother?" Red Hood called, standing at the threshold. The house usually smelled of clove and rosemary, but today it smelled of blood. "Grandmother, are you all right? I've brought you some medicine."

"Oh, wonderful!" a rough voice howled from her grandmother's bedroom.

"Grandmother? Is that you? You sound awful."

"It's me, dear. I'm just so sick. I'm not myself."

Red Hood swallowed, sensing something amiss.

"Did you happen to bring any wine? I'm so thirsty. Go on and bring me a glass. I'm far too weak to get out of bed."

No one had taught Red Hood what the twisting in her belly meant. She ignored the warning and poured the glass of wine, her hands trembling.

"Hurry, girl," the voice ordered.

As Red Hood tiptoed slowly to the back of the house, she could hear breathing coming from her grandmother's room.

"Grandmother?" Her tone was faint with fear.

"Yesss."

The room was dark, with just a thin beam of dusky light coming through the window and falling on a hairy brow.

"Grandmother…" Red Hood stopped. "Your eyes…"

"All the better to see you, dear."

She stepped closer, squinting into the shadows.

"Your ears…"

"All the better to hear you, sweet child."

Red Hood took a last step forward, now so close to the bed that she could see this was the wolf from the road wearing her grandmother's dress. She knew the wolf must have eaten her grandmother, and she knew her life had never been in greater danger.

"Your teeth!" she wailed as loudly as she could, and a hunter passing by heard her scream.

"All the better to eat you with!" The wolf grabbed the girl and devoured her whole just as the hunter burst into the room. The beast snarled and crouched, moving to strike the man, but the hunter's blade had been drawn and the wolf leapt straight into the knife; it pierced his throat, and he fell down dead.

Acting quickly, the hunter carefully made a shallow cut down the wolf's belly, and little Red Hood crawled out, gasping for air. Together, the girl and the hunter dug through the beast's swollen belly and pulled out the grandmother.

The hunter tried to revive her, but to no avail.

"She's gone," he said. "I'm sorry."

Red Hood, suddenly full of rage that this beast had tricked her, refused the hunter's words.

"No, she's not." The girl pressed her lips to her grandmother's and exhaled long breaths into her mouth. She refused to quit and, finally, her grandmother coughed and opened her eyes.

And they lived happily ever after, made so, as we all are, by gratitude and grief.

The Three Rites of the Red Hood

Now that we've arrived at the ever-after, what do you still wonder? In your journal, take note of what seems to be a missing piece from the story and turn it into a question. You might ask, for instance, How could the girl mistake the wolf for her grandmother? Your questions might point toward something you feel is wrong with the story, a hole in the plot or a vital piece of wisdom that somehow has been lost in transmission. Try not to overthink your question; let the first query that steps forward be the right one.

Now, having named the question, ask, How is this the very question of my life? In other words, how is your question about the story actually about your life right now? Trust the intelligence of the story to show you exactly what you need to see right now in this moment. Turn the question about the story into a question about your life. It could be simple, such as, What am I afraid of? Or it might be more complex: What wolves have I mistaken for grandmothers? Trying not to overthink it, name your life question.

Now look to your message from the haunted woodland that you wrote down before the story began. When you envisioned the haunted woodland, you allowed that image to speak. What did it tell you? Now ask, How is this message from the haunted woodland an answer to my life question? Look to this question-and-answer pairing, your life question and the message from the haunted woodland, and allow this to orient you as you begin the Rites of the Red Hood.

In our guiding story, the haunted woodland is a threshold place, a shadow ground between the life that was and the life that will be. In a traditional indigenous rite of passage, the young wanderer must face death, encountering a formidable ordeal, in order to become new. There can be no birth without death, and for this reason the beasts must come close enough to terrify us, even swallowing us whole before our inner warrior sets us free. In a rite of passage, we must believe — even if only for an instant — that we cannot make it out of these brambles alive, and there in our horror, we allow the old self to die so the wiser self might be reborn.

Red is the color of magick in the old stories, but it is also the color of blood. We find Red Hood on the cusp of adolescence in our story, at the time of her first bleed, and she is given a great task at this time, to carry medicine from her mother's house to her grandmother's house, to become part of the ancestral story and, in so doing, to face the wolf in the woods.

Rite I: A Mythic Signal

Look to your life question, the question born from the story, as well as your lesson from the haunted woodland. If your question was *What am I afraid of?* and your lesson was *Let the darkness heal you*, what small act might you do, a small rite you might perform in order to let the darkness heal you? Perhaps you will name a dark room sanctuary, lighting a lone candle to represent your fiery skull, and sitting in a state of presence for as long as you have. Perhaps you will go for a meaningful walk through a woodland, looking at the places where the shadows fall and seeing what you can see.

A rite is a ritual. Remember that the original meaning of the word *rite* is "to observe carefully," and we must approach rites with great care. Consider your haunted woodland lesson a clue, a mythic signal orienting you toward the next step in your story. Move through this rite just once, allowing it to change you somehow, not rushing through it. Script this moment into your story. After you move through this first rite, ask yourself one last question: What must die so my wiser self might live? This might be a limiting belief, a relationship that strangles your liberation, or a persistent fear that once served but now constricts. Write your answer down on a piece of paper not bound in a journal. Place this piece of paper on your altar until you are ready to complete the second rite.

Rite II: Losing the Way

In life, as in the old stories, an initiation follows three discernible phases. Of course, the experience of a lived-out-loud initiation has no clear steps between this and that, no boxes to tick or objectives to meet. We always begin with a severance, a death, and a shedding of skin. This is the threshold moment. There was before this, and now there is after this. Following the severance is the void, the liminality, the deep and timeless space between death and birth, and, last, if we learn what we must learn, we find renewal.

These initiatory stages have been reframed for the feminine experience as containment, metamorphosis, and emergence, and we witness them in Queen Inanna's ancient myth from Sumer as descent, void, and ascent. In many fairy tales the severance happens when the innocent crosses that original tree line, in pursuit of quest or rest, and the great work of initiation gets done in that dark forest, in the liminality between what was and what will be. Only after their time in the wildlands do they emerge wiser, remade by their underworld journey. Our soul is rendered through our initiations, through these three-phase experiences of becoming new, of losing our way in the wilderness and being reoriented toward an unexpected destination where our wiser self is born.

The young person's early rite of passage, evident in numerous cultures the world over, follows a similar but intentional process. The innocent leaves their old world behind to face death, to encounter an unpredictable ordeal that permits them deeper communion with their soul's voice. Only after believing they would die there in that wild place can they return, being welcomed home by their people, given a new name, and seen as worthy of wisdom. In fairy tales this universal adolescent rite is made visible through the innocent's impossible quest, often tasked to the youngest of three siblings, and we learn much about our own initiatory experiences when we return to these haunted woodlands where the next possibilities in life are seeded, where the strangest futures are suddenly available to us.

Little Red Hood stays close to the road, but she does lose her way for a while. She forgets the urgency of her task and begins to slip through time. Sometimes losing our way is necessary, a hallmark of the initiatory experience. After the severance, the leaving of home, there can be no going back to the way it was before. If the way itself is hidden, if the way is lost, then we are sure not to return until our transformation is complete.

When you're ready, when it feels right, sense the call. Maybe you look out your window to see the trees bending to the wind's will in such a way that you know it's time. Maybe there's a song in your heart pulling you from the warmth of your house. When it's time, before you head into the world, safely burn your piece of paper bearing the name of that which must die. Carrying the ashes, walk in solitude. Ponder your many initiatory experiences.

When have you been swallowed by your own shadow, the very thing you ignored, the very beast you swore did not exist? Your dark shadow is who you would swear you are not, the hidden monster who is formidable only in its invisibility.

When has your inner warrior come to liberate you from the belly of the beast and, in so doing, also freed the foremothers who could not free themselves? How are you mending your lineages simply by carrying the medicine, by wielding your inborn gifts, learned wisdoms, and acquired skills? How are you healing your grandmother just by breathing?

Ponder these questions as you walk, feeling no pressure to arrive at a clear answer. Like Red Hood, lose your way for a time, if you can. When you're ready, find a hidden place, take a breath, and scatter the ashes to the wind.

On your way home, imagine yourself moving toward a new desired chapter in your life. Perhaps you can see this next chapter with great clarity, or perhaps much still feels elusive. Be soft with yourself. Bear witness to the visions that come, and ponder the image of the Red Hood.

Rite III: Stitching the Ancestral Hood

In the time when folk fairy tales were being collected and literary fairy tales were being written, one of the most fearsome characters to the patriarchy was the weaver-woman. The term *spinster*, used as a derogatory label for an unmarried older woman, originated in an effort to condemn the successfully self-employed woman who did not need financial support. Spinning and weaving were good trades, and these women did not need to marry in order to survive. When women gathered to work, as they often would when weaving or spinning, such a gathering was feared by the overculture for its otherworldliness, for its hidden nature where anything could happen outside the watchful eye of male authority. In *From the Beast to the Blonde*, Marina Warner writes, "Typical meeting places for women alone, like public laundries and spinning rooms, were feared to give rise to slander and intrigue and secret liaisons. Of all the professions, official and unofficial, those which allowed women to pass between worlds out of the control of native or marital family seemed to pose the greatest threat to apparent due order." To weave has always been the witch's work, and witch's work has always threatened the powers that be.

When you feel ready, consider how you might create your own ancestral hood, a wearable symbol of your unique ancestral medicine, the gifts from the grandmothers to you but also from you to your forebears. Let it be something you craft. If knitting, sewing, and weaving are not in your practice, you may just find a length of red fabric and draw sacred symbols on it with a permanent marker. You may already have a red hat, cloak, or hood you can transform for this work. Let this rite feel liberating. Let it meet you where you are.

With your chosen materials gathered, call to mind the symbol of the Red Hood from our story. Call to mind the sacrifices of the grandmothers, your own healing gifts, and imagine yourself as ancestor. Some wild child nine hundred years from now is calling on their ancestor and sees you just there, stitching a red hood, dreaming of what comes. Some fairy tales are more than five thousand years old, so maybe, just maybe, this future ancestor has also met this enduring story, envisioned little Red Hood, pondered the dark beauty of the haunted woodland, and encountered the wolf on the road. Create your ancestral hood with these peculiar possibilities in mind, and sense your story as just one breath in the long ancestral story.

When your ancestral hood is complete, breathe into it. Consecrate it with your breath. Now it becomes a magickal object, a sacred symbol of your belonging to something greater than the small story, from this day until forever. Speak a spontaneous incantation into it, and wear it well.

Crossing the Mossy Threshold

Animating an old story full of wisdom and wonder changes you. After moving through the Three Rites of the Red Hood, notice how nature begins to participate in and even shape your experience. What strange synchronicities do you notice? What portals did the story open for you that were not named in these pages? What has come alive in you that lay dormant before? Who are you now, and what feels like your most important knowing from your work in the Night House so far?

If you feel called, mark this moment. Stand at a threshold in your house, a space between two rooms where, ideally, there is a door. Wear your ancestral hood. Place both hands on the doorframe, close your eyes, and imagine you are standing at the edge of the haunted woodland, the dark forest at your back and the rising sun before you. Sense the bark under your hands. Breathe deep. Freely speak aloud for as long as you have, beginning with the following words: *I have been to the haunted woodland, and now I know…*

Be witnessed by your loving ancestors, by the creatures of the woodland, and by your wise and future self. Be held by the energies inherent in the story, and welcome the many possibilities that come. Here you find a before-this-and-after-this moment, a threshold hour in your story. Here you are ready to move deeper into the Night House, holding the bleeding key, opening the red door, and stepping across the threshold into your next once-upon-a-time.

Chapter 2

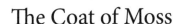

The Coat of Moss

Let your craft be rooted in the words of our ancestors but make them your own... Follow the guidance of your familiar spirits. Let your craft be both old and new, preserved and renewed through your efforts. Such forms of craft can never be stagnant or flakey, for like a tree, they reach deep into the ancient dark in order to shoot forth in new growth, straddling the line between what has passed and what is yet to come.

ROGER J. HORNE, *The Witch's Art of Incantation*

The term *fairy tale* was not used until the late seventeenth century, yet some of these wonder stories are believed to be many thousands of years old. The magick housed within such stories is easily dismissed by those who may not recognize the structure and intent of a spell, but for those who do, spellcraft abounds in fairy tales. In these tales are spells that save and end lives, yes, but also that fulfill destinies, spiriting the innocent from the too-small life to one that supports their wholeness. The etymology of the word *fairy* finds a source word in *fate* and, while a fairy may not exist in every fairy tale, fate is always afoot. Better to call them fate tales, stories of transformation, integration, and healing despite life's limitations.

While destiny liberates us, fate binds us. A destiny is, at least in part, chosen, while fate is the lot we were born to. In Greek mythology the strange women who are the Three Fates, the Moirai, are feared and revered, and rightly so, for they alone spin a life and cut its thread. Clotho begins to spin the thread at one's birth, Lachesis measures the thread, and Atropos cuts the thread at death. In Norse mythology, the three Norns keep the World Tree alive and weave the grand tapestry of life. In the old stories, fate, like a story, is woven. We weave a tale. We spin a yarn, and, in that hallowed space between the once-upon-a-time and the ever-after, we are contained within a hand-knit house of meaning, bound by a certain fate.

The spinner-women, those spinsters who dared to defy cultural norms and support themselves, were feared not only for their financial independence but also for their gatherings, their congregations created in spinning rooms where fate tales were spun alongside the woolen yarn. The word *gossip* originally referred to close friends who gathered, particularly in birthing rooms or for christenings. While gossip would later be condemned as women's talk, idle and meaningless chatter that is devoid of purpose, the word once connoted shared communion, often through storytelling, in spaces where men and wealth were absent. Who knows what the world's fate might be if it is truly woven outside the gaze of the most privileged eyes?

Of course, if these stories had been more rightfully called fate tales, they might have been taken more seriously and therefore their tellers hunted, hanged, or burned at the stake. While fairy tales have at times aroused the suspicions of the powers that be, as a mere children's story, as idle talk that has no purpose, such a story is safe from the king's decree, too unimportant, too inconsequential for the tellers to be pursued and imprisoned. We might wonder, though, how aware the weaver-women were of their mythic role. Surely the archetype, the original form, of the spinning sisters who weave the world into being was alive on the tongues of these spinsters. Surely their fate tales were wielded for greater ends than merely passing the time, and surely more than a few of these weavers were witches.

A witch is someone who holds the old wisdoms, the word itself derived from *wicca*, meaning "craft of the wise." A witch practices witchcraft, a practice whose definition has shapeshifted considerably over the years. Few lineages have been left unbroken, but the spirit of the witch lives and thrives. While spellcasting need not be the purview of every witch, it certainly is for many contemporary practitioners, and to cast a spell is to raise energy toward a specific intention, to create an energetic container of meaning that is not unlike a story.

When a storyteller tells a tale, they enchant their audience for a time. They create conditions where those who are meeting the story are, in part, bound to the conditions they present but, more accurately, to the conditions presented by the story itself. A storyteller is a channeler, allowing the breath of the tale to come through them, to spill from their tongue like honey wine or bile, to allow the strange braid of teller, story, and witness to be superior to any one of those singular participants. For that reason, every time a story is witnessed, it shapeshifts to best meet the moment.

Invitations for Tale-Tending:
Fate, Place, and Wickedness

The walls of this room in the Night House are covered in an enchanted moss that whispers your name. Hold the tension of the impossible as you meet this story, as you begin the second lesson of the Night House. As before, consider that, just maybe, it is no coincidence that you are reading this story today. Perhaps you were destined to meet the girl who dwells inside the house of moss, who was gifted a spell by her mother and sets out to meet her own fate, to wed her wildest self.

Attend to the themes of home and desire, the kinship between place and fate, and also consider the voices of the "wicked ones," the women from the kitchen. *Wicked*, like the word *witch*, references wisdom and, for all their faults, the wicked sisters in the old stories do hold their own wisdoms, which we will consider more deeply in the three rites following the tale. Notice the images from the story you sense are important, images that seem strangely to have their own vitality, and seek validation for the Night House's second lesson: The Otherworld participates in our everyday experience.

The Otherworld participates in
our everyday experience.

Before we meet the girl who dwells in the house of moss, consider the wild image of a garment, a coat, intricately stitched, made entirely of moss in all its many colors and textures. How do you see this mossy coat? Can you breathe it in? Does it have a sound, a song? Meet this mystical garment with all your senses, writing or drawing a description of the coat. Then ask yourself: If this image could speak to me now, what would it say? Write down the answer, your message from the Coat of Moss.

STORY ALTAR: THE MAGICK OF MOSS

Stories appreciate these houses we build for them. Before you meet the story, if you feel called, gather some moss for your altar. Alternatively, spread a green cloth. Speak a spontaneous prayer to one of your land teachers, a place you visited once or many times, a place where you sensed the spirit of the elements, a place that felt alive in wild and unseen ways. Imagine this place now as you build your altar. Whisper heathen poetry to the dirt and the trees, the sand and the mountains. When you are ready, light a lone candle on this altar, and ready yourself to meet Mossy Coat.

The Coat of Moss

Once in a time that was always, never, and now, there lived and breathed a little girl who dwelled with her mother inside a house of moss. No one remembers quite how it happened, but though once made of wood, stone, and thatch, the house grew a cloak of shaggy green so thick that it pierced the walls. Like moss itself, the house became a rootless wonder, having no foundation or support to speak of yet holding its shape and going on living just the same.

The little girl grew up inside her pillowy, earthen house, and her dreams were of faraway lands and drier weather. All the while, she longed for her mother's attention. Even when the girl was quite young, her mother stayed locked away in her room, always mysteriously busy and never inviting her daughter inside to see what kept her away for so many hours. The older the girl grew, the more absent her mother became. Parented only by the moss, the little girl feared what might become of her.

One morning, just before the girl was about to turn nineteen, she woke to the sound of a man rudely shouting for someone to come speak with him. All around her the moss seemed to ripple and hiss in warning, but she went out to meet him anyway. A red-faced peddler he was, carrying bags of trinkets and gadgets.

"Ah, well, aren't you a pretty one!" he bellowed, eyeing her up and down. She frowned, saying nothing. "My, my, my." He clicked his tongue. "I think it's my lucky day."

"What do you want?" she barked, backing up behind the threshold and wishing her mother would come out of her room to save her.

"Well, I was going to try to sell you a few pots and pans, but...I believe my intentions have changed."

She backed up even farther, and he stepped closer. In that moment, the moss seemed to form tiny, jagged points that were sharp to the touch. He rolled his eyes around the strange house, his expression at once disgusted and impressed.

"Surely, you have no suitors to speak of," he half muttered. "I mean, living here all alone."

"I'm not alone," she corrected, pulling her shawl tightly around her shoulders. "My mother is here."

He seemed disappointed and tried to peer into the house behind her. "Well, I don't see her."

The girl swallowed, and the moss around the threshold pricked up like thorns.

"Mother or no mother, I'd like to marry you."

Her breath caught in her throat, and suddenly she was without a voice. All around her, the moss crackled and spit, weeping water around her feet.

"I...I," she managed, shaking her head. "I must speak to my mother."

She left him there at the threshold and rushed to her mother's room. He tried to follow her, stepping inside, but as soon as his foot touched the ground beyond the doorway, the shaggy green ground swallowed his foot whole, and he was stuck.

Meanwhile, the girl was calling for her mother, begging for her to come out.

"What is it?" the mother called and finally showed herself, annoyed.

"There's a man here, an awful man. He wants to marry me. What do I tell him?"

The mother's face fell in an instant, but then she composed herself. "Tell him to return in seven days with a gift. The gift should be a white-and-gold dress that fits only you, and the gold must be real gold."

"But what if—" the girl started.

"Just go," the mother said and vanished.

The girl told the peddler to bring her the dress in seven days, and he agreed; as soon as he did, the mossy ground gave way and freed his foot so he could leave.

The girl spent those seven days praying to the moss that he not return, and her mother stayed in her room. Never before had her mother stayed away so long, and the girl was quite lonely and forlorn.

One week after his first visit, the peddler returned with the white-and-gold dress, and the girl was terrified.

"I've room for you in my cart, my love. Let's be off!" He reached for her, and a piece of the mossy roof fell on his head.

"Wait here. I must speak with my mother," the girl said, taking the white-and-gold dress and rushing away.

Again, she cried for her mother to come out and, when she did, she looked quite bothered at the interruption.

"Put that dress in your room and tell him to return in seven days with another dress. This one should have every color of every bird that flies in the sky and, of course, it should fit you exactly."

An impossible task, to be sure, thought the girl. The peddler was angry that he was being sent away again, but he agreed. For the next seven days, the girl prayed to the moss, and her mother stayed away.

Two weeks after his first visit, the peddler returned to the house of moss with the many-colored gown, and the girl's eyes grew wet with tears. She brought the dress to her mother, having to call for her for more than an hour before she would leave her room.

"Put that dress in your room and tell him to return in one week with shoes made of silver that fit you exactly," directed the mother, and she was gone.

The peddler was enraged now, sure the girl was tricking him.

"You have no mother!" he howled, reaching for her, and the moss began to rattle and shake all around. He backed away. "In one week, I'll return with those silver shoes, and you're going to leave with me and be my wife."

The girl spent that week praying to the moss to save her, full of a newfound ire. Her mother should protect her, after all.

Three weeks after his first visit, the peddler returned with the silver shoes, and the girl left him at the doorway and cried for her mother.

"Go into your room and put on the white-and-gold dress, along with those silver shoes. Go to him then. Let him see you. Tell him to return in the morning, and you will leave with him as his bride to be. He will be too dumbstruck by your beauty to argue."

"But…but I don't want to leave with him," the girl protested, and the mother shushed her.

"Go!" she ordered, disappearing.

Her mother was right. As soon as the peddler saw the girl dressed in his gifts, he could barely speak, managing to mutter only "tomorrow," nodding, and backing away from the house without taking his eyes off her.

That night, the girl sat weeping by the hearth dressed in her gown, and the moss wept with her. She fell into an uneasy sleep, knowing it would be her last night in the house of moss and dreaming of a wild man with dark eyes and warm hands, a strange man she had never seen before and yet somehow knew to be her fate.

When she woke, it was dawn, and her mother was at her side, stroking her hair.

"Oh, my darling girl," she whispered. "I have something for you." She helped the girl to stand and bid her close her eyes.

"I know you think I was bad at mothering, but allow me to give you this last gift."

The girl opened her eyes. There, in her mother's proud hands, was a lavish coat made of green-gold moss, so carefully stitched, so painstakingly crafted. The girl couldn't help but weep when she saw it.

"When you wear this coat, you can wish yourself to be wherever you like. You can wish for your desire to come true, and the moss will make it so."

The mother began helping her daughter into the peculiar garment. "I began making it the day you were born, and I finally finished it this morning, my last stitch as the sun began to rise."

As soon as the coat was fully on her body, the girl could feel herself beginning to drift through time and space. She could hear the voices of her ancestors and unborn children. She sensed the greatness of her story, of her one lone chapter in the grand book of wild women.

"Wish yourself to be wherever you like," her mother said, blinking a lone tear from her eye and handing her the many-colored dress. They could both hear the peddler's cart rolling toward the house. "Forget your old name. Your new name is Mossy. Go now, my girl. Go!"

The girl hugged her mother with all the might she had and then wished to be at a grand house in a faraway land where she would meet her destiny. She felt herself coming apart and being put back together again. She was in communion with deep time, with all that ever was or would be. When she could feel her feet on the ground again, she was at the end of a long path that led to a great house. She wasn't sure how much time had passed, but she felt older and quite wise. The shining sun turned her coat a bright gold, and she looked a wealthy woman when she knocked on the door of the grand estate house.

A woman answered, and the girl was suddenly full of boldness.

"My name is Mossy, and I've come here looking for work."

The woman was impressed by this strange woman on her doorstep and agreed to let her work in the kitchens. She showed her to a glamorous room — much too posh for a kitchen servant's room — and told her she'd introduce her to the kitchen staff that night and to make herself at home in the meantime.

In a closet larger than her childhood room, Mossy hung her many-colored dress and her coat made of moss. She stared from her window down into the gardens below. Full of hairy, bright moss, these gardens were, lush with trees and a mirror-still pond at the center of it all. She wept with a great knowing that she could find belonging anywhere if only she looked.

Suddenly, dropping from a low branch of an apple tree, a wild man appeared in the garden and stared up at her. She recognized him from her dream the night before but ducked away before he could see her.

Full of joy, Mossy twirled into the kitchens later that night. She was sure she would be great friends with whoever worked there, that she would be well welcomed.

"This is Mossy," the woman of the house announced. The servants — three women with vicious eyes — eyed her silver shoes and white-and-gold dress. "Treat her well."

Of course, they didn't. Almost immediately the women in the kitchen were cruel to Mossy, scorning her fancy clothes.

"Who do you think you are?" they said. "Living in the main house with your room overlooking the garden? Pah!"

They gave Mossy the filthiest work that night and, by the time the sun set on this, her initiatory day, Mossy's dress was covered in ash from the bread ovens, red sauce, and cooking oil. The silver shoes were tarnished and stained. Her face was smeared with ash and soot, and her hair was stuck through with food they'd thrown at her. She went to the garden to cry, lamenting the state of things, and the moss heard her.

"What's the matter?" It was the wild man from her dream, from the garden earlier that day.

Mossy wiped her eyes, smearing the ash and soot, and waved him away. She didn't want him to see her like this.

"Well," he started. "This is my house. If there's anything I can do to help, just ask."

She curled to sleep on the moss that night, leaving her grand bed untouched, and asking for a telling dream.

In her dream she was walking through a sea of sleeping bodies toward the wild man. Her mossy coat was whispering *sssstayyyy*, and she woke knowing she couldn't leave. Not yet.

For a few weeks, day after day, she endured the cruelty of the three women, trusting her dream and the wisdom of the moss that brought her here. When she saw the wild man, it was always at the end of the day when she was covered in ash; he never saw her face.

One night, on the cusp of the summer solstice, she had another dream.

This time she was dancing with the wild man and the mossy coat was whispering *today*.

When she woke, the house was abuzz with activity, and she learned there was to be a grand ball that night. She set to work in the kitchen, but before she could receive any orders or insults, the woman of the house approached.

"Mossy," she started, scowling at the three cruel women who were eavesdropping. "My son and I would very much like you to join us at the ball this evening. You don't need to work. Not tonight."

Mossy saw the women glaring.

"That is, if you would like to join us," the woman of the house added, looking down at her filthy dress. "I could give you a gown to wear."

Mossy saw the women smirk in her direction, and she wove a plan in the space of a few breaths.

"Actually, if it's all the same to you, I think I'll decline. Thank you, though."

The cruel women shared glances, surprised.

"Suit yourself." The woman of the house left, and Mossy excused herself quickly, running upstairs to her room.

There she pulled the rainbow gown from her closet and spread it out on her bed. Then, with great care and a prayer of thanks to her mother, she wrapped the mossy coat around her shoulders, breathing it in.

"I wish for my silver shoes to be as they once were," she said, and it was so. "I wish for the three cruel women to fall into a long sleep right now, not waking until dawn comes," and it was so. The women fell to the ground asleep, with pots bubbling and bread baking.

Mossy, meanwhile, crept into the gardens and bathed in the clear pond, whispering to the water and the lilies that today was the day. Careful to stay hidden, she snuck back to her room and put on the rainbow gown, silver shoes, and golden moss coat, braiding her hair and thinking of her more innocent days.

When she heard the music begin to play, she left her room and joined the merry crowd in the ballroom. Everyone wondered where the food and drink were, as no one had discovered the sleeping servants, but Mossy was still in the corner of the room, eyes locked in desire with the wild man's. He had never seen anyone so beautiful. She was strangely familiar, but he had never seen her without ashes on her face, so he didn't recognize her. Even so, he believed this glamorous stranger to be the love of his life.

They danced together all night, Mossy and the wild man, and it was just as she'd dreamt when she was back in the house of moss. They barely spoke, but they knew of their shared fate.

At midnight Mossy pressed her hand into the wild man's chest. "I must go," she said. "Find me," and she stepped out of one of the silver shoes and ran into the shadows.

The wild man picked up her shoe and ran for the door, thinking she must have left for her home, but really she had gone to her room in his house.

The next morning, the three cruel women were fired for falling asleep and leaving the guests without food or drink.

The wild man put the word out that he was looking for a woman whose foot would fit the silver shoe and, before noon, there was a line of women from all over the countryside waiting to try on the shoe. For hours and hours, each woman tried to fit the shoe but failed. Mossy watched from her room for three days while her wild man searched for her in the sea of strangers.

Finally, as dusk fell on the third day, the wild man wept as the last woman left, and Mossy put on her mother's handmade coat one last time. "I wish for that wild man to see me as I truly am, always. May he love me well, as I love him, and may there never be a lie between us," and it was so.

She came out of her room, finding him in the garden and slipping her foot easily into the silver shoe. He recognized her immediately, and they, of course, lived happily ever after, made so, as we all are, by gratitude and grief.

The Three Rites of the Moss

Like the missing pieces from a dream, what feels to you like glaring absences after an old story ends can be just as telling as the more obvious lessons from the tale. Now that our guiding story is over, what questions remain? What are you still wondering about this wonder story? In your journal, write this question down. You might wonder what became of the peddler or whether the maiden ever wore the coat again. Name the question.

Now consider this: You might have asked any number of questions about the story, yet this was your query. Why? How is this the very question you hold in your heart right now? What does this question tell you about your own fate, destiny, or purpose? As before, turn the question about the story into a question about your life. *Did she ever wear the coat again?* might become *What do I need to reawaken my own magick?* Dig under the question about the story, and mine the deeper question about your life. Try not to overthink it, and name your life question.

Now look to your message from the Coat of Moss that you wrote down before the story began. How is that message an answer to your life question? Let this question-and-answer pairing, your life question and your Coat of Moss message, orient you toward what you must see as you begin these, the Three Rites of the Moss.

Rite I: Moss Scrying

Holding the tension of your life question and its answer, the message born from the mossy coat's mythic image, go into the wild if you are able. Find, if you can, a patch of moss. Alternatively, find grass, a dandelion stretching up through concrete, or anything at all that grows.

When you are ready, fix your eyes on the moss, on what is green and growing. Let your gaze soften. Here you are looking, but you are not looking. Here your inner narrator ceases to speak and, if you give yourself just a few minutes, there will be wide spaces between your thoughts. In these spaces, allow a new question to step forward.

This is a question that seems to crawl out of the moss, a strange question that may stun or surprise you. The question might seem mundane, a question about what you are seeing when you gaze at the moss, or it might seem to bubble up from some hidden well inside your psyche. Whatever your question, when it emerges, write it down. Offer gratitude to all that grows, even, like moss, rootlessly, and complete the rite simply by asking yourself this: What wish and what worry are housed within my question? If you prefer, you might ask what desire and what obstacle are present, tucked inside the query itself.

Sometimes the wish and the worry are obvious, and sometimes you must peel back a few layers of language before you get to the beating heart of what wants to be seen. Perhaps you asked why there is gold at the edges of the moss patch but a deep green at the center, for instance. Maybe you asked whether moss can speak, or where the lushest parts of your own life are. In the first example, the wish might be for gold to come from the sun and the worry might be that the golden moss is actually dying. In this rite, in this ritual, the question itself is the oracle. Whatever wish and worry step forward for you to witness are important.

In preparation for the second rite, hone your wish and your worry so they feel quite close to your heart, vital parts of the current chapter in your story. What do you wish for? What do you desire? Name this, then ask, What feels in the way? For what do I worry, and how does this worry impede my wish?

Rite II: Away with the Wicked Ones

The wicked voices in the old stories, whether they come from the stepmother, stepsisters, or, in Mossy's case, the women from the kitchen, can reflect back to us the voices of our inner limiting protectors. These voices always get louder when our art, whatever our sacred work is in this life, is about to be witnessed. The exact language of the wicked ones varies but almost always relates to something akin to this: *Who do you think you are?*

Who do you think you are to write that book? Who do you think you are to plant that beautiful garden or get on that stage?

These voices tend to be boring, as they are not nearly as creative as the inner artist, but they are there making themselves heard nonetheless. In preparation for the second rite, consider your worry or your obstacle that emerged from the first rite. Does that worry point you toward the voices of your own inner wicked ones? The voices of the wicked ones are quite familiar and, strangely, are often the same no matter what you are creating.

On a piece of paper, write down between one and five of these statements from the inner wicked ones. You might say: *No one will want to read what I write* or *I don't know enough to create this.* Sometimes they are truly vicious, these voices, but more often they wear the guise of the helper. They might suggest you return to school before you do your work in the world. *You need more training,* or *this is not going to make you any money.* Remember that at the root of *wicked* is *wisdom*, and there may well be truth to what these voices say. In the end, though, you know that if this is your purpose, your "object to be kept in view" throughout your life, any voice that tries to keep your great work from being witnessed does not deserve your attention.

These wicked ones often emerge during childhood when we so boldly finger-painted, hand-crafted mudpies, or recounted a dream as if it were the greatest story ever told. Maybe our miraculous art was belittled or shamed, maybe we simply learned we'd receive more attention if we devoted our time to other pursuits, or maybe it was not safe to be seen as creative or curious. We likely cannot know the circumstances surrounding the birth of these inner wicked ones, but we recognize when we are fighting a battle we did not start, when we are still guarding against a threat that is no longer present.

When you feel ready, breathe deep. Invite your loving ancestral spirits to come closer, and, in a burn bowl or cauldron, burn the paper bearing the words of the wicked ones. Watch the smoke rise. Notice what you see in the flames. When the fire cools, gather the ashes and place them on your altar in preparation for the third and final rite.

Rite III: Glamouring Desire's Coat

A glamour spell imbues a seemingly everyday object with meaning, enchanting magick into the mundane, inviting the Otherworld to sing through the day-to-day experience. The magickal garment, like the Red Hood, is a hallmark of fairy tales, and it speaks to the ways of the witch. A glamour spell might be wielded to enchant an object in such a way that others perceive the wearer differently. For the third rite, you will enchant an object so that you perceive yourself differently, as needed.

In my own offerings and trainings, I often invite participants to create their own "wild skin," a sacred shawl or shapeshifting pelt. When the wild skin is worn, it does not move its creator into a new shape; it merely brings them closer to who they already are. We may not want to show our untamed self, our "wild skin," to the world for all to witness, but we do want to be able to slip into it from time to time, to remind us why we are here, and why now.

The invitation now is for you to create your own "coat of moss." As with the Red Hood, this could be a garment you already own and will now repurpose, or, if you have some of the spinner's blood, if you embody a bit of the weaver-woman archetype, feel free to create your own. Let the garment bear some of the color green if possible, giving a nod to our story, but the rest is up to you. Consider your wish from the first rite. What wild skin speaks to this wish?

Once you have your coat of moss, consider now how you would like to enchant this garment. What do you need to believe about yourself in order to see your wish come to fruition? This belief might be the opposite of what the wicked ones say. It might be: *My art is worthy* or *my words have power*. Name this belief, the belief you want to have when you wear this wild skin.

When you are ready, invite the ancestors and the spirit of the four directions in. Hold your coat of moss to your heart. Whisper your new belief out loud, and imagine a version of you is standing just in front of you, their back to you, who is already wearing this wild skin, who already believes the words you just spoke with their whole body. Breathe with your witch's breath into your wild skin and, when it feels right, wear your coat of moss and take one step forward, stepping into the version of you who already, fully and wholly, believes your words.

Offer gratitude to the otherworldly ones who participated in the rite with you, and then carry the ashes from the wicked ones' voices into the wild. Throw them to the wind. Turn, and do not look back. When you wear your coat of moss in the coming days, you will begin to embody the belief more fully. Wear this, your wild skin, when you create, when you ready yourself to be witnessed, when your gifts are screaming to be seen and heard.

Meeting the Shapeshifting Woman

Stories make us curious about the impossible. They soften our hard-edged understandings about who we are allowed to be and, by extension, what our world is becoming. The story of the Coat of Moss challenges our notions about time, determinism, and what some might call "wishful thinking." In a fairy tale, the presence of magick is not only required; the whole story unfolds around its presence. When we meet a story full of wonder, a part of us senses the truth of the Otherworld, the possible within the impossible. The wild skin — and indeed the Red Hood and the Coat of Moss — become just as real as our own flesh.

After you move through the Rites of the Moss, notice the shifts that occur in the coming days. A shapeshifter moves and morphs into a form that lives closer to what they desire, nearer to what they have come to love. When you feel ready, mark your transformation by standing at a threshold, wearing your coat of moss. Breathe deeply and, when you are ready, freely speak without editing yourself, beginning with these words: *I have worn the coat of moss, and now I know...* Be witnessed, be heard, and be seen, ready to move deeper into the Night House, ready to learn a greater truth about the wild skin and to meet, again and for the first time, the shapeshifting woman. She's part creature and part human. She's befriended her less civilized nature and, if we let her, she just might remake our world.

Chapter 3

The Swan Maiden

*In human lives, stories precede normal guidance systems, and stories
continue to function when normal guidance systems have failed. Stories
bring their share of grief; companionship with them is by no means
entirely benign, and those who ignore their dangers will probably end
badly. But stories also reenchant what becomes disenchanted...they
open a door to the next world. Those who seek to banish stories because
of their dangers will never know that reenchantment is possible.*

ARTHUR FRANK, *Letting Stories Breathe*

Some chapters in our lives inspire us to ask ourselves, Who is my
inner wild one? What nourishes them, and what can they teach
me today? A part of us is less civilized than the overculture would prefer, and for certain our foremothers shared the same tension between
needing social acceptance and harboring an inner untamed self. The
stories of shapeshifting women show us the truth of our living paradoxes: stability versus freedom, roots versus wings. In the old stories
this paradox sometimes translates to mother versus creature, wife versus animal, the tamed housekeeper versus the wild woman.

Many of us met at least one old story for the first time through the
image of Mother Goose, an apparently benign matronly figure who
housed hundreds of stories in her heart, but this old wild mother is

partly a reference to women's hidden desires, desires that could be expressed in birthing rooms and midwiferies, spinning houses and other women-only places, night houses where watchful eyes could not see clearly. The association of the stork with birth paralleled the emergence of this Mother Goose, with waterbirds closely associated with women's less civilized nature, specifically as it was expressed through voice, "gossip," and storytelling. Marina Warner writes, "Mother Stork's part in storytelling moves along two axes: how she communicates (her clatter, her chatter) and what she talks about (her naughty claptrap). This folklore does not belong in the classical tradition of myth; it grew up at the childbeds, the lying-ins, the bedrooms and the nurseries of more recent history." In Dutch, the author notes, the words for women's chatter, *clapperij*, and the sound a stork's bill makes, *klepperen*, are closely intertwined. Bird-women were dangerous women, in other words.

The hidden rooms where women worked, birthed, and healed were, to the outsider's mind, like another world, a world where they were not welcome, an invisible world where anything could happen. These hidden rooms were dangerous places where, like the so-called witches who crept away at night to worship the devil and fly on broomsticks, women were believed to shapeshift into another, far less proper form. In the hidden rooms, marriages were undone, true paternities were concealed, secrets were spilled, and of course, stories were told.

Waterbirds like storks, geese, and swans became associated with such unladylike behavior, the dirty talk and the ruder wisdoms. The stories of shapeshifting women then take on a greater power when these old tales show women transforming into these foul fowl incarnations. The wild skin becomes a pelt of feathers, and the uncivilized bird-woman becomes both the coveted object of desire and the dangerous animal who cannot be caged; if she were, beware the broken heart that would inevitably follow.

Invitations for Tale-Tending: The Wisdom of Wildness

The air smells of autumn rain here in this new room in our hidden house. A white feathered pelt lies draped on an altar, and the mist-spirits haunt every corner. Just for now, consider that you are meant to invite your inner wild one to come a little closer today. For some reason, your less civilized self wants to be witnessed right now, this telling hour, and they wish to be witnessed inside an old story. As you begin the third Night House lesson, stay curious about your own shapeshifting nature, about what it means to be a human animal.

Consider your experience with the first two lessons in this book, with the Red Hood and the Coat of Moss. In this story we shall meet an even wilder skin, the feathery pelt. Begin by holding the tension of a personal paradox. Ask yourself, What two roles do I play that seem to not sit well together? When you embody one of these roles, you feel as if you cannot play the other at the same time. You might say scientist and witch, provider and artist, mother and lover. You may long to play one of these roles all the time and feel you are making a sacrifice to be playing the other. One of the roles likely feels more liberating, while the other seems limiting or confining. Similarly, one of your roles might seem more socially acceptable than the other. Name your personal paradox now.

As you meet the story of the Swan Maiden, tend to the themes of wisdom, wildness, and loneliness. Notice the duality between the shapeshifting woman and her hunter. Stay attuned to the image of the feathery pelt, and be curious about your lived encounters with your wildest nature. You might ask, as our story unfolds, which of your two roles wears the feathery pelt, the wild skin, and further, to whom do you give permission to see your pelt, to dare to touch your more creaturely shape? What conditions do you require to let your uncivilized self be seen? Here we consider the third lesson of the Night House: There is a time and a place to wear the wild skin.

There is a time and a place
to wear the wild skin.

Before we encounter our Swan Maiden, see now the image of a pelt of white feathers. How do you see this pelt? Where do you see it, and what other colors are present? What season is it, and what sounds

45

do you hear? Meet this, our third wild skin, with all your senses. Draw or write a brief description of what you sense, and then ask, If this feathery pelt could speak to me now, what would it say? Write this down, your message from the pelt of feathers.

STORY ALTAR: ODE TO THE BIRD-WOMEN

If you feel called, build an altar to this old story. Let it be an altar to the hidden wisdoms, to your inner paradoxes, and to your own power to move between the worlds of the civilized and the untamed. Let your building of the altar be a symbolic action, an ode to the bird-women. "Emblematic signs of the goose and stork," writes Marina Warner, "like the webbed foot or the long beak, recur in synecdoche to denote female sexual knowledge and power, as well as the implied deviancy which accompanies them; the sirens who lured men on to the reefs with their song were also bird-bodied and web-footed." Include on your altar symbols of your wilder wisdoms, your hard-won understandings that few would want to hear, that even fewer would accept. Give a nod to the bird-women, and let your altar be an ode to your inner shapeshifter.

The Swan Maiden

Once upon a full Blood Moon, a lonely hunter wept beside a wild mountain lake. He feared another long winter spent without a woman, he lamented every choice he had ever made, and by midnight he considered walking into the water and never returning. Sleep came for him before he could put a permanent end to his sorrow, and a telling dream soon found him.

In his dream a silver-skinned woman with white feathers for hair rose from the lake and sang a haunting song. When he woke, dawn was looming, the lake was cloaked in mist, and he was humming the song from his dream, fresh tears pooling in his eyes.

"What is becoming of me?" he whispered, sensing every once-impenetrable wall around his heart softening.

Just then a shadow encircled the lake, then another, then another. The hunter held his breath while three great swans descended from the brightening sky and landed so lightly in the water they made no sound. The sun began rising, and all was quiet for a time.

The lake was cast in a golden light, and the hunter pressed his hand to his heart. Just then the three birds' wings grew long, their eyes widened, their backs straightened, and there, standing in the water, were three feather-haired women. On the shore not far from where the hunter sat were three white-feathered pelts.

For hours the hunter watched while the creaturely women swam and played in the water. So struck by this sight was he that he wondered if he was still dreaming.

"Let me not wake," he prayed aloud, recognizing the smallest woman from his dream.

When the sun began to sink low in the sky, the hunter watched the women, one at a time, pull their feathery skins over their shoulders, crouch into the water, return to their swan forms, and take to the sky. As the last woman, the silver-skinned shapeshifter from his dream, rose high in the sky, he hummed the song from his dream and fell asleep.

That night, he dreamt of his long-dead mother. He was curled in her lap as if he was a babe again, whimpering and telling her of the swan maiden. His mother smoothed his hair and hushed him.

"Tomorrow, when she returns, swipe her feathery pelt. Tuck it away, and she will stay with you for a time. In seven years, you must return what is hers," his mother said, then she began humming the swan maiden's song.

The hunter woke the next morning to the sound of laughter, and again he saw the three beauties swimming and splashing in the water, their white feather skins resting very near to him. Remembering his mother's words from the dream, he leaned close to the skins and snatched the smallest one, the one he knew belonged to the woman from his dream, and he hid her wild skin in a nearby cave.

Hours passed, and the hunter wondered if he'd done the right thing.

"Do I deserve this?" he wondered out loud as dusk came creeping. "Do I deserve you?"

The silver-skinned woman began singing the song from his dreaming time, and the hunter leaned closer to the water, waiting. The two other swans returned to their creaturely form and took to the sky, but the smallest woman searched the shore as the full moon rose high. She stopped her song. He could hear her breath quicken, and only then did he step from the shadows.

"Come home with me," he whispered, and her black eyes met his. She bowed her head, understanding her strange fate, and he covered her with his coat, leading her to his woodland hut.

For seven years, the swan wife and the hunter lived well in love. She tended the wilder part of his heart, and he tended the tamer part of hers. Each morning, she would watch the birds fly, her face full of longing. Each night, she would swim in the mountain lake, humming her soul-song. Every full Blood Moon, the hunter would wonder what would happen when the time came to return her feathery skin.

At dusk on the seventh anniversary of their meeting, the hunter hoped against hope his great love would stay with him, and as she swam in the lake at moonrise, he pulled her pelt from its hiding place while she sang her song.

"Will you stay?" he asked, handing her feathers to her. She looked at him with pity but said nothing, stretching her feathers all around her and returning to her swan shape. Without a word, without a sound, she took to the sky.

The hunter sat waiting for her on the banks of the lake, not eating or drinking, his eyes fixed on the sky. He remains there to this very day.

The Three Rites of the Wild Skin

Our story ends without a traditional happily-ever-after, as we know many stories do. Now that our tale is finished, what do you still wonder? In your journal, write down just one question about the story. You might ask, Did the Swan Maiden know she was going to leave the hunter? Or, Were the pelts of the swan sisters also stolen before our story began? As always, your question can be anything. Let a seemingly small question about the story step forward, and make note of it.

With our previous two Night House stories, we have allowed our question about the story to become a question about our lives. Now we allow our story question to grow larger than us, to speak to the world story. Breathe into your question, and let it grow. How is your question about the Swan Maiden story really a question about the world story? Write a new question now, a question we will call the "world question." Last, look to your message from the feathery pelt, the message you wrote down before our story began. Is this message somehow a strange answer to your world question? You might have asked, for instance, When will the lonely hunters of the world stop stealing wild skins that do not belong to them? Your answer, your message from the feathery pelt, might be, *For now, protect me.* Whatever your question and answer, allow this pairing to give you ground as you begin the Rites of the Wild Skin.

Rite I: Flying Between Worlds

Call to mind your personal paradox, the inner duality you named before meeting the Swan Maiden in the story. Ask yourself to consider which of these two roles feels less tamed, more creaturely, and more likely to wear the wild skin. Now ask, If this role was an animal, what kind of creature would it be? Last, in preparation for our first Rite of the Wild Skin, ask, Where does this animal live?

Go to a place where this creature might live, either literally or in your imagination. Stand, if you are able, and allow your palms to face skyward, bending your elbows slightly, and begin to gently shift your weight from one foot to the other. Breathe easily, and let the rhythm be slow.

Consider now that you hold your wilder role in your left hand. When you lean to the left, as much as you can, fully embody this role. If your wilder role is "wise woman," for instance, when you lean to the left, you are fully and *only* wise woman. Notice how you hold your body, how you breathe. Ask yourself what it would be like to be only this. What do you wear as that wild one? How do you spend your days?

When you feel ready, begin to consider that when you lean to the right, you embody the other role, the one that may be more stable, predictable, and socially acceptable. What is it like to be only that? What changes do you sense in your body?

Stay with this, shifting slowly from one role to the other, imagining yourself transforming from this to that. Begin to quicken your pace when you feel called. Begin shapeshifting more readily from the tame to the untamed, the palatable to the deviant. Begin flying between worlds.

As the rhythm quickens, you might begin to sense that a third energy is present, a third road opening between this and that, an energetic invitation to hold the tension of both roles at once. Take care with yourself, as this work can be intense, but begin to sense the *both* as the power source. You are not this and then that; you are both at once. You are all.

Notice any signs you are receiving from nature, from the weather, from the creatures that slither and fly. When you feel ready, begin to slow the rhythm down once more, again sensing the separateness between your two roles. Take your time. When you feel returned, when you feel a sense of greater wholeness and your feet are firmly planted on the ground, come to stillness, and notice how you feel. In your journal, you might write a short reflection on the sensation of *this, that, and all*, noting how the third road looked and felt. In the coming days after you complete this first rite, notice the moments when you feel you must choose between *this* and *that* and, in those moments, recall the energy of the *both*, of the third possibility, the often hidden third road.

Rite II: The Shapeshifter's Dreaming Time

In solitude, when the time feels right, consider what it would be like to spend a year living only as your wilder self. Whatever season you find yourself in now, begin there. If it is springtime, for instance, ask yourself how your less tamed self would spend their days in spring. What time do they wake? What morning rituals do they keep?

Recall what it felt like to be only your wilder role during the first rite. How would you spend your hours if you were only that? Consider these questions and, if you feel called, write in your journal a sensory description of how your wild self spends a typical day within each season. Let the description be present tense, as if it is already happening. Begin with the words *I am*.

When you are ready, if you can go into a wild place, go. Remember that wild does not necessarily mean unbuilt or uninhabited; it might be a fringe place where you feel strangely at home, a somehow forbidden ground where, for some reason you do not need to name, you can be witnessed by the Otherworld. Go there, and read your writing out loud. Notice the signs you receive, the strange synchronicities that resource this work. Feel free to animate your writing, to move in ways that reflect your words. Become creaturely. Crawl and howl, run and hiss.

In the hours and days that follow, afford attention to your dreams. Tend to this question: Who am I becoming? On your altar, place an object that represents your wild self, that reflects your experience in the first two rites.

Rite III: The Wild Knowing

In preparation for the third and final Rite of the Wild Skin, consider the difference between your two roles once more, but this time tend to the ways in which their beliefs about the world differ. Perhaps your inner wild one believes the world is inherently good, for instance, while your more civilized self is pessimistic. Maybe your untamed self believes the world exists outside linear time, or that time itself is an illusion, while your more civilized self believes linear time is necessary. Name a belief that your wild self knows to be true but that your more tamed self questions or maybe does not believe at all. Write this belief down.

Over the next three days, actively look for proof that this belief, this wild knowing, is true. The proof can come from anywhere, from the show you are currently bingeing or the words your friend said to you, from a dream or a memory. At the end of each day, make a list of the proof you have gathered. If you feel called to continue after three days, stay with the practice for nine days, then perhaps thirteen, and then, last, if you are able, making it all the way to twenty-one days.

Whether you stayed with the practice for three days, twenty-one days, or any duration in between, notice what begins to change in your life. Is there an area that seems more affected by this work than others? Do other wild knowings want to be embodied more fully?

You might reflect on your original question-and-answer pairing from before you began these three rites. What was your question about the world, and what was the answer, the lesson from the feathery pelt? In reflection, ask, How does the wild belief I worked with speak to my question about the world and the feather pelt's answer?

Waking the Shadow Twin

In the end we understand the dangers of becoming only the wildest version of ourselves. We know parts of us do not want to be witnessed. When we consider our inner shadows, however, we are not considering what we know about ourselves and consciously hide from the world; we consider those parts of us that exist outside even our own awareness. Many of us live closely to the inner wild one. We wear our wild skin often, and we may even permit a few to see us wearing it, but even the wildest among us fear the shadow, our inner twin whom we might call sinister.

Keep track of the small changes and strange signs, those cosmic nods you receive from the unseen realms after you complete the Rites of the Wild Skin. Notice what and who activates you in the day-to-day world, especially when you are not alone. What about the more civilized world causes a visceral reaction in your body, a charged sensation? Notice what you feel oriented toward now, and when you feel ready, complete your work with the Swan Maiden story by crossing a threshold — a doorway, a bridge, a narrow stream, any threshold will do — any sacred place that seems to say *there was before this, and now there is after this*. After you cross the threshold, freely speak a small prayer that begins with these words: *I have worn the feathery pelt, and now I know…*

Move deeper into the Night House now, and ready yourself to meet the Shadow Twin, the most vicious monster that lurks in the dark recesses of our psychic underground.

Chapter 4

The Shadow Twin

If one lived quite alone, it would be practically impossible
to see one's shadow, because there would be no one
to say how you looked from the outside.

Marie-Louise von Franz, *Shadow and Evil in Fairy Tales*

Fairy tales are not without peril. These stories are full of trouble, wrought with hazards that threaten to break apart our carefully built belief systems — about ourselves, our people, and our world. Some stories might just remake a person, disturbing them into letting the old self die so the new self might live.

Part of the fairy tale always operates in the dark, inviting the shadow self to step forward and dance with one's light-of-day personality; this means permitting who you refuse to be, who you would swear you could never be, to sit close to who you think you are. Through this peculiar and fated encounter, you become someone your younger self may not even recognize. The severed bits of you are stitched back together. You become more whole, and the shadow self blinks at the dawn's light for the first time.

To integrate our shadows, we consider the parts of us we have subconsciously deemed both too bad and too good to ever show the world. Ecopsychologist Bill Plotkin calls these aspects of self the *sinister* shadow and the *golden* shadow. Our dark and sinister shadow is like the foul flower in our guiding story; it is viscerally repulsive, a monstrous reflection of the personalities we find the most problematic. Our golden shadow is like the bright flower in the story, a shining beacon of traits we find desirous, powerfully seductive, even holy.

Fairy tales have a way of not only weaving the dark with the light but also permitting them to coexist, to interact with one another in a way they do not, in a way they *cannot*, in our everyday experience. The story provides a container for integration, for a sort of psychic healing we witness in that hallowed space between the once-upon-a-time and the ever-after. In an old wonder story, we become all we have refused to be but might yet become. We are the villainous wizard and the wild maiden, the vicious witch and the lost child. We become the shine and the shadow, the bright and the foul.

Invitations for Tale-Tending: Death Sits in the Room

Our new room in the Night House is full of flowers, some full of sweet-smelling beauty and an equal number full of foulness and rot. This story is our last tale before we descend into the Night House's bone cellar, the place where our tales become a bit darker, where our medicine becomes more bitter, where death sits in the room with us. As we prepare for this descent, consider this initial question: Who could I never be? As you invite the tension of the fourth lesson in the Night House to sit with you, begin to name who you refuse to be, who you would say you could never, ever be.

Recall your paradox work from our last chapter. Remember those twin dualities you named that illuminated your tame self and your wild self. Your dark and bright shadows, these foul and bright flowers in our guiding tale, may seem like amplified versions of your tame and wild selves. Approach this work with curiosity. Stay playful, and stay wise. In the beginning don't take yourself too seriously, and here's why: As soon as you name parts of your shadow, as soon as you consider their integration, they are already no longer your shadow. The shadow is what is not conscious, and therefore inviting the shadow to be seen already requires transformation.

Naming what is both too *bad* and too *good* to be you invites change, so take great care. Begin by considering the characters from stories, stories you know well, old stories and new stories, fiction and nonfiction, to whom you seem to have a visceral, embodied reaction. Who are the heroes and the villains that seem to create a strange charge in your body and, most importantly, what is it about them? Why do you adore or despise them? This is just an initial inquiry, but be kind to yourself as you do this work. Even these small questions can sting deeply. The charge in the body tells you that you are coming close to a new truth.

When you meet our guiding story, the tale of Tatterhood, tend to the imagery that speaks to the light and dark, the bright and foul. Tend to the many dualities of characters housed in this single story: the foster princess and the little beggar child, the prim and proper queen and the wild witch on the mountain, the bright twin and the Shadow Twin. Notice the theme of integration as the story unfolds, and consider our fourth Night House lesson: Name the ghosts that haunt you, and their power becomes yours.

> *Name the ghosts that haunt you,*
> *and their power becomes yours.*

Before we meet the bright and foul twins, call to mind the wild skins we have met thus far, the Red Hood, the Coat of Moss, and the feathery pelt. Now we will encounter the tattered hood. How do you see this tattered old hood? What color is it? Encounter this hood with all your senses. This is the fourth wild skin, the last magickal garment we will wear, the final piece in our Night House wardrobe. In your journal, draw or write a brief description of this tattered old hood, and then ask, If the tattered hood could speak, what would it tell me? Write this down, your message from the tattered hood.

STORY ALTAR: THE SHADOWED SELF

Tatterhood is a story that wants an altar. This is an altar to your shadowed self, the part of you that houses your greatest and as-yet-unseen power. Building the altar is a symbolic action of inviting the shadow to swim toward the surface. Include symbols of the bright and foul flowers, the beauty and the rot. Let your altar enchant and revile, seduce and repel.

Tatterhood

Once in a time that was and was not, there lived a king and a queen who were blessed with great wealth, power, and celebrity. They had everything they had been told to want in life, and though they were envied by many, their abundance could not buy them the one treasure they truly desired. Try as they might, the king and the queen could not have a child.

For years they prayed for a child that never came. While the king slowly but surely accepted their plight, the queen refused to believe motherhood was not part of her fate. In her most brilliant daydreams, she saw a babe at her breast. In her midnight dreaming time, she walked the castle's gardens with a beautiful golden girl, but, alas, she could not become pregnant.

With every new moon came her blood. With every bleed came her deepening sorrow. Vexed by her childlessness, the queen's goodness began to die. Worsening her anguished state was the wild fertility of the queen's sister who, on the eve of summer solstice, gave birth to her thirteenth child. Full of rage, the queen was. Her sister was nothing, after all. Her sister married a pauper and had no wealth to her name. What right had her sister, a poor woman with no title, to bear so many children when she, the queen, was left childless?

In her desperation, the queen went to her sister's birthing bed and demanded she give her one of her children.

"You have so many, dear sister," the queen reasoned. "Surely you can spare a daughter. The age of the child doesn't matter to me, and I'll be sure to give her a better life than you ever could."

In her weakened state, the queen's sister agreed, sending her nine-year-old daughter away with the queen to live at the castle.

That very night the queen, for the first time, had a terrible nightmare. She dreamt of a creeping demon child who rode a black goat and wore a tattered gray hood. In her dream she could hear the goat's hooves knocking slowly through the hallways of the castle, and she woke terrified that some great terror was coming for her niece. Breathless, she ran to the little girl's room to find her asleep and well, but from that moment on, the queen became fiercely protective of her niece, the little foster princess.

Though it was a sunlit and rainless summer, the queen refused to let the little girl play outside the castle's walls. She trusted no one, and the more rigid the queen's rules became, the darker her demon-child nightmares grew. The worse her dreams, the more protective of the foster princess she became, and by July's full moon, the queen's niece was allowed outside her room only for an hour on Sundays, and she spent that hour playing in the courtyard under the watchful eye of the queen.

That year, First Harvest — that holy day nested precisely between summer solstice and the autumn equinox — fell on a Sunday. It was a day when the ghosts were always afoot, the queen knew, but her nightmares the night before had kept her from sleeping soundly. Even so, she couldn't remember exactly what it was she'd dreamt.

She was red-eyed and weary this day, that queen. She had tried to keep the foster princess from playing outside at all, but the princess had begged, saying summer was nearly over and the weather was to be so beautiful. The queen agreed but cut her playtime, allowing her to be outside for only a half hour while she watched from the tower above.

While her niece played with a doll in the courtyard below, the queen struggled to keep her eyes open. It happened all at once. A servant slammed a door loudly in the hallway, the queen spun around toward the sound, her eyes settled on the red door to her bed chamber, and she remembered the horror of her dream from the night before.

In her nightmare the hooded demon child was opening the door to the queen's room and riding her goat straight toward her bed, twirling a splintered wooden spoon and howling like a wolf. The queen gasped at the memory, breathing a sigh of relief that it was only a dream, but when she looked back out her window at the courtyard, the foster princess was gone.

Frantically, the queen looked everywhere, pressing her hands and face against the glass. Where had she gone? The memory of her dream quickened her heart and her breath, making her think the worst. In her mind the demon child had come to carry her niece away. As soon as she had that thought, she saw her.

Near the castle gate, she was, and she wasn't alone. The foster princess, dressed in a pink silk gown with the sun glinting off her golden braids, was playing with another child, a dirty beggar. The queen was disgusted. The other child had a filthy face and torn clothes, and the two of them were tossing a golden apple back and forth.

"Get away from her!" the queen cried, and pounded on the window, but the children were so far below they could not hear. Gathering her skirts, the queen tore out her bedroom door and down the tower's many stairs.

Meanwhile, the two little girls were playing catch, giggling, and sharing a little conversation.

"Do you live here at the castle?" the little beggar child asked the foster princess.

"I do. I'm the queen's niece, but she's raising me as her own," the princess answered.

"Oh," said the beggar child, and she furrowed her brow. "That's strange."

"It is," the blonde girl acknowledged. "And you? Do you live here at the castle?"

"Oh, no," the dark-haired girl answered. "I live on the mountain with my mother. She's a witch."

"A witch!" The foster princess was delighted. "What sort of witch is she?"

"She's a fertility witch," the beggar child answered matter-of-factly. "She helps the babies get born."

Just then the queen ran out of the castle, screeching.

"Well, I should be going," the beggar child said, frowning at the fast-approaching queen, and she disappeared.

"Who was that child?" the queen demanded, shaking the foster princess. "You aren't to play with anyone! Do you understand? Did you tell her who you were?"

"Yes," the foster princess answered calmly. "Don't worry. She was very nice, even though she was the daughter of a witch."

The queen was always repulsed by witches and wrinkled her nose. "Oh, how horrible, a witch's child. Let's get you into the bath."

Later that night, the queen was brushing the foster princess's hair and, for reasons she did not know, asked her niece, "Did that child tell you what sort of witch her mother was?"

"Yes, she said she was a fertility witch," the little girl answered casually. "She helps the babies get born."

The queen let out a slow exhale. From that moment on, she couldn't stop thinking about the mountain witch who maybe — but couldn't possibly, but maybe, but no, but perhaps — could help her have a child. By September's equinox she had decided to set aside her distaste for witches and invite the mountain witch and her daughter to come to the castle for dinner.

The feast was grand indeed, and the foster princess and the witch's daughter played catch with the golden apple in the hallway while the queen and the witch sat at either end of a banquet table so immense they had to shout to hear each other.

"So, witch," the queen started as the first course was served, "you probably already know that I invited you here because I've tried for years to have a baby. I know you can help me, so give me a fertility spell. I'm your queen, and I order you to give me a spell that will work."

The witch smiled at first, but her smile turned into a loud cackle that shook the walls. "No," she said finally. "I'm afraid I can't do that."

The queen stood and walked toward her, full of rage but composing herself quickly and grabbing the wine bottle.

"Very well," said the queen. "It couldn't hurt to ask. Have some more wine."

After the third course had been cleared, the queen had poured more than two bottles of wine into the witch's goblet, and she dared to ask again. "Witch, listen. I'm queen. I can give you land, title, money, anything you could ever want. Surely you're tired of living on the mountain. Your daughter could wear fine clothes, eventually marry a nobleman, and have a brilliant future. All I want in return is that fertility spell."

The witch didn't laugh this time, looking at the queen with pity, and slurring, "I don't want your money, queen. I'm not giving you the spell because I know your kind. I know you'll break the rules, and if you do, the spell will ruin your life rather than bless it. I'm not giving you the spell in order to protect you."

Again, the queen was furious but did not show her true feelings. She nodded in feigned grace and poured the witch even more wine.

It was nearing midnight, the last course had long been cleared, the two little girls were asleep in the hallway, and the witch was resting her head on the table and singing softly.

The queen swallowed, walked to the witch, and knelt on the ground at her feet.

"I beg you," she started, beginning to weep. "I beg you. A child is all I want, all I've ever wanted. I would give up all I have if I could just give birth to a daughter of my own."

The witch raised her head, suddenly sober, thought for a moment, and sat back in her chair.

"Very well, I'll give you the spell," she conceded, and the queen wiped her tears, clapping and smiling. "But you have to do everything exactly as I say. Do you understand? Exactly as I say."

"Yes, yes, I'll do everything exactly as you say," the queen agreed, standing.

"On winter solstice, the longest night, you will go to the holy well in the woods. Do you know it?" The queen nodded. "You must go yourself, and you must go alone. Do not send servants. Bring no guide with you. Go yourself, and bring two pails to fill with the well's water. Carry them home and invite the king into your bed. After you lie with him, send him away, wash yourself in both pails of water, then put them underneath your bed. In the morning you will wake to find two flowers growing under your bed.

"One of the flowers will be the sweetest-smelling, most brilliant and vibrant bloom you've ever seen, and the other will be the foulest oozing flower that's ever grown in this wild world. You must eat the bright flower whole. Do not even touch the foul flower. Leave it be, for in a few days it will rot and turn to dust. You will know you are pregnant before January's new moon."

The queen listened intently, understanding all the witch said.

"You must do it all exactly as I say," the witch reminded her. "Do not break any of the rules. It must be winter solstice, you must go to the well yourself, and when those flowers bloom, eat only the bright flower."

The queen agreed fervently, thanking the witch and sending her and her daughter away. The next morning, she sent the foster princess home to her sister, full of faith that the spell would work.

At first she was committed to obeying every rule, but by October's end, she knew she couldn't wait until solstice. On the day of the dead in early November, she sent her servants to fetch two pails of water from the well in the woods. That night she invited the king into her bed and washed in the water, keeping that part of the spell true, but the next morning when she woke, when she found those two flowers under her bed, she ate the bright and beauteous flower as she was told but — and no one knows why she did it — after she swallowed that bright flower, she ate the foul and stinking flower whole. The rules were broken.

By the January new moon, just as the witch had said, the queen knew she was pregnant, and by First Harvest, the anniversary of the foster princess's first encounter with the witch's daughter, the queen was in labor. The midwives were terrified, knowing that if this child wasn't born healthy and well, the queen would be devastated and it would mean their heads, so they were relieved when the queen pushed just once and the most beautiful, shining child emerged from between her legs.

Everyone in the room wept, knowing how long the queen had waited for this moment, seeing how healthy the child was, but a few moments later they heard it, the drumming. Where was it coming from? The queen was cradling the bright babe on her breast and smiling, but the low rhythm was filling the room.

The oldest midwife, the one who had seen such things before, put her ear to the queen's womb and, without any warning, another child was born. The midwives gasped and leapt back from the birthing bed as the newborn babe rode out of the womb on a goat, wearing a dark hood, howling, and waving a wooden spoon in the air.

The queen was so disgusted at the sight of the hooded child, the very child from her nightmares, that she retched. This chaotic scene went on for more than an hour, with no one knowing what to do, watching the strange creature ride around the room.

Finally, the queen managed to order the child be caught. "Get rid of it!" she screamed, cradling the bright babe closer, but every time the midwives tried to get the Shadow Twin out of the room, the bright babe began to scream as if in great anguish. It quickly became clear the two could not be separated, the bright twin and the foul one.

For years the queen conspired to send the Shadow Twin, the daughter they came to call Tatterhood, away from the castle. She tried to send her to the witch on the mountain, blaming her and her spell for the demon child's birth, but just as it was in the birthing room, the two girls could not be separated without the bright twin wailing in great pain.

Tatterhood seemed to have knowledge of the old ways. As the twins grew older, Tatterhood would spend her time in the woods gathering plant medicines and speaking to the dead. The bright twin was always at her side, learning and witnessing.

One night, the longest night, in fact, the castle was attacked by an undead horde, the wild hunt, a band of screaming banshees and vicious otherworldly creatures. Perhaps they came because the queen had broken the rules so many years ago, as this was the ninth anniversary of when the queen was supposed to have cast the spell, or perhaps they were there for another reason, but the king, queen, and their two daughters hid in the tower and waited for fate to find them.

Finally, Tatterhood rode her goat to the door, waved her wooden spoon, and said, "I know what to do. I'll save us. Whatever you do, do not let my sister leave this room." The king and queen agreed, and Tatterhood went down to meet the creatures of the night.

Worried for her sister, the bright twin couldn't wait. When the king and the queen weren't looking, she crept down to the castle gate and pressed her ear to stone, hearing Tatterhood's howl and believing she had won the battle. Without patience, the bright twin opened the castle door and Tatterhood screamed, "No!"

An undead witch snatched the bright twin's head off her body, replaced it with a horse's skeletal head, and disappeared into the dark. Tatterhood was furious. Her parents had let her sister fall prey to the otherworldly beasts, and now her sister's head was gone.

The queen fell into a deep depression, for now her bright child was also foul, her beauty and innocence gone. Both her daughters were ugly, and she lamented the whole of her life, that queen.

On the eve of her daughters' seventeenth birthdays, the queen sat silent at dinner with her family, as she often did now.

On this night Tatterhood spoke with great authority. "I believe I know how to recover my sister's head, but you must let us go alone. You must prepare a great ship with no crew and allow the two of us to go together alone to the sea."

The queen, who once had been so protective of her niece, agreed in her softened state. She allowed her daughters to sail off together the very next day with no servants, no sailors, and no hope of their return.

Tatterhood sailed them both straight to the witch's island, and there on the shore was her sister's head on a pike.

"You have to go on your own to claim your head," Tatterhood said to the bright twin, and though the bright girl was terrified, she swam to the shore and grabbed her head, replacing it with the horse's head, and then straightened her own head on her neck and smiled.

The bright twin felt older and bolder, somehow full of wisdom she had never had before.

"I don't want to go home yet," she said, and Tatterhood smiled.

"Good, let's keep going."

The two of them sailed for years and years, seeing foreign lands and meeting wild people. In time they sailed past a castle where a great king and his son lived. The king watched while a ship sailed by. On the deck stood a hooded woman riding a goat, and with her the most beautiful woman he had ever seen.

"Bring them here!" he ordered his men, and soon enough the twin women were standing before him. Instantly in love with the bright twin the king fell.

"Will you stay?" he asked the bright twin.

"It's up to my sister," she said, and Tatterhood smiled.

"Very well. We'll stay for a while," Tatterhood agreed, and the twins stayed at the castle for a year while the king fell deeper in love with the bright twin. Finally, on the eve of their twenty-ninth birthday, the king proposed to the bright twin.

"I will marry you," she agreed, and the king smiled with great joy. "But only if your son marries my sister."

The king knew his son would not be happy, but he was so in love with the bright twin, he agreed.

Such a weird and wonderful wedding, the four of them had. The twins felt whole and well in a way they never had before, dancing farther and farther away from each other as the celebratory music played on.

As it neared midnight, the full moon shone overhead, and the bright twin said to Tatterhood, "I think it's best that we spend some time apart, just for a little while. We've never been apart, after all."

Tatterhood agreed, and the next day Tatterhood rode off on her goat with the prince at her side. The prince looked quite despondent, of course.

"Oh, prince," Tatterhood grinned. "You look so sad. Why don't you talk? Ask me why I ride this goat."

The prince frowned, resigning himself to a life with this woman, and obliged her. "Very well, Tatterhood. Why do you ride that goat?"

"Is it a goat?" Tatterhood asked, grinning and suddenly riding a majestic white horse.

The prince was impressed but still plainly upset.

"Why don't you ask me why I carry this wooden spoon?" Tatterhood asked after a few hours of traveling.

"Very well," conceded the prince. "Why do you carry that wooden spoon?"

"Oh, is it a spoon?" Tatterhood asked, suddenly holding a brilliant bejeweled wand.

The prince couldn't hide his admiration now, and he smiled. They rode on for another hour before Tatterhood asked another question.

"And prince, why don't you ask me why I wear this tattered old hood? I was a princess, after all. Don't you wonder why I wear such a thing?"

The prince asked earnestly, "Yes, why do you wear that tattered hood?"

Suddenly, the dark hood she had worn her whole life, that had been born with her and had grown with her, disappeared, and she was shining brilliantly, looking like the bright sister's identical twin and wearing a golden crown.

"Is it a tattered hood?" she asked, and the two rode into the amber sunset together to live happily ever after, made so, as we all are, by gratitude and grief.

And so it is.

The Three Rites of the Tattered Hood

In this Norwegian fairy tale, there is a trinity of shadow twins, six characters who seem to both repel and amplify one another. The pristine queen is made whole by the mountain witch, as is the bright twin by the foul twin, the foster princess by the beggar child. Now that our tale is finished, what do you still wonder? In your journal, write down one question about the story. You might ask, Did the queen ever see the witch again? Or, What exactly were the bright and foul flowers under the queen's bed? Whatever you wonder, write it down.

As we have done with our previous stories, with our previous questions that followed the ever-after, ask, Why is this my question? How is this the very question of my life right now? Whatever your question about the story, transform it now to be a question about your life. Permit your question about the Tatterhood fairy tale to become a question that feels suddenly, strangely even more personal. We will call this our shadow question.

Look now to the lesson from the tattered old hood, the lesson you wrote down before our story began. If you allow this lesson to be a peculiar answer to your shadow question, what do you notice? Let this question-and-answer pairing orient your approach to these, the Three Rites of the Tattered Hood.

Rite I: Eating the Bright Flower

In the beginning of our story, the queen is plagued by shadow dreams. In *Women Who Run with the Wolves*, Clarissa Pinkola Estés notes that a woman's shadow dreams often precede a great creative awakening. Whatever our art, whatever our sacred work in this life may be, this personal purpose is always nourished by the shadow's gifts, the treasures you came into this life with. Before these gifts are made conscious, they haunt you in the hidden corners. They creep and crawl wherever they can be witnessed, often in unhelpful places. They distract, they cause us to obsess, and they torment our day-to-day lives.

In the story we might name the first duality encountered as the barren queen and the fertile sister, with the queen's sister being very like her bright shadow, embodying the shining gift she wants with all she is but cannot express. The mountain witch is like the queen's foul shadow, embodying the sinister and the grotesque, the dirty and the forbidden. When she eats both the bright and the foul flower, the queen is acting to integrate both shadowy shapes, the part of her that was too good to ever be her and the part that was too bad to be her. She gives birth to these shadows, gestated in her psychic womb, in a new form, Tatterhood and the bright twin, her shadow daughters.

In your journal, begin this rite by returning to the character traits you find admirable, viscerally desirable. Consider the celebrities, artists, and even politicians you might admire. You intellectually understand these people are flawed and wounded, but the shadow operates outside our intellect, hidden from our inner narrator who understands the role everyone plays, who continually gives an understandable story to our experience. For this reason, it is best not to overthink this question: What traits do you viscerally admire in other people?

The list you make now describes your personal bright flower, your shining shadow. When you feel ready, fill a vessel — a glass, a goblet, a mug — with water or another drink of your choosing. Invite your loving ancestors to come close, to resource you in this moment. Speak a soft prayer over the vessel, and then, when you are ready, imagine a strange, mythic embodiment of your bright shadow qualities. Conjure an image of one character or creature who fully embodies the entirety of your list.

Spontaneously, begin to describe this bright flower character, naming the traits you have listed as well as any others that might surface, letting your words spill into the vessel. When it feels right, breathe three powerful exhales into the vessel, and then drink all the liquid therein. This is a symbolic action, a small ritual, of eating the bright flower, of mining the gold from the hidden places, of coming to an embodied understanding that you are *that*.

Rite II: Eating the Foul Flower

Unlike the queen in our story, allow some time to pass between the first and second rite, between the ritual consumption of the bright flower and of the foul flower. When you are ready, return to the list of traits you find viscerally repulsive, the descriptors of villainous personalities you find grotesque, monstrous, even obscene. You believe these traits do not belong in your world, maybe not even in the world at large. You feel a visceral charge in your body when you encounter people who seem to embody these traits, and you would wholeheartedly swear that you are not anything like the horrid creature you describe.

You are not that. Say, for instance, you name laziness as one of your foul flower traits. Shadow integration does not mean proclaiming you have been lazy all along; it means looking for what gift may be under the "laziness," your right to rest, perhaps, that you may have hidden away during childhood because you received and internalized input that this treasure — your right to rest — was somehow bad or even dangerous. In her book *Eastern Body, Western Mind*, Anodea Judith describes the shadow's evolution as akin to a tasty lunch you brought to work one day but tucked inside a drawer and forgot about; now it is moldy and it reeks, but it began as something nourishing and healthy.

For each of the sinister traits you name, consider what gift might lie underneath it. For example, weakness might be vulnerability, stupidity might be your ability to ask questions and not know every answer, and self-centeredness might be the ability to steer the direction of your own life. See if you can name a hidden treasure for each repulsive quality, and create a new list of the foul flower's treasures.

When you are ready, as before, fill a sacred vessel with a liquid of your choosing. Try to not use the same substance as you did with the first rite. Invite your ancestors and otherworldly helpers to come close and bear witness. Begin to imagine a mythic character who embodies these treasure qualities. Who are they? How do they dress? How do they make you feel?

Begin to speak your foul flower's treasures list over the vessel. Speak as if you are casting a spell, slowly and with intention, as if time does not exist. Don't rush. Take care. Remember, the wild unseen is with you now in this moment. Exhale three breaths into the vessel then, and drink. As with the bright flower's rite, this is a symbolic action of inviting the dark shadow's treasures to come forward, to step into the light for the first time in a long while.

Rite III: Feeding the Wilder Self

At the end of Tatterhood, the Shadow Twin reveals herself to be identical to the bright twin. Women often have negative reactions to the way this story ends, as if Tatterhood was somehow polishing herself to be more palatable to the prince, as if she was sacrificing her greatest source of power; these responses are valid, of course. As with the questions that remain after the story ends, however, there is often value in considering why you feel the way you do about the end of the story. What sort of ending might you script instead?

In preparation for the final Rite of the Tattered Hood, look to your lists of bright flower traits and foul flower treasures. For certain you will feel closer to embodying some attributes on these lists than others, especially given certain circumstances and available resources. Get weird now and imagine a mythic character who embodies the traits of both lists fully and completely. Who are they, and what do they look like? Draw them in your journal if you feel called to, or simply imagine them as real.

Now, even more strangely, consider what an ideal day in the life of this character would look like. How do they spend their hours? What feeds them?

Now consider one seemingly small action that you can reasonably take, ideally in less than an hour, that would be part of this character's day. It can be anything and need not be an action that seems completely outside your normal day-to-day life. Maybe this character mindfully drinks their tea every morning, for instance, or tends their altar at night. Name this action and, when you are ready, commit to doing it once a day for three days. This might be an action you already do, but now you will do it with a different and specific intention: to consider yourself this mythic character, if only while you drink that tea or tend to your altar. Whatever your decided action is, commit to moving through it for three days in a row and, while you move through this, your Rite of the Wilder Self, you will imagine moving as your bright shadow moves, embodying the gifts of the darker shadow and noticing how you feel.

Over the course of these three days, notice how nature joins you in your experience. What is the weather doing? Is there a song in your head that won't leave — and then you hear it inside the wind? Make note of bizarre synchronicities and strange happenings. Discount nothing. If you notice it, it likely has value. Take note, and reflect on your shadow work experience, your work with the tattered old hood.

Entering the Bone Cellar

Stories that house a definable shadow invite us to consider who we are not. The traditional villain in a story may not necessarily be a reflection of our dark shadow, however. Conversely, many of us might remember sensing a kinship with the "wicked witch," with the powerful sorceress from our childhood cartoons or the ferocious Baba Yaga. Intuitively, we understood the power embodied in these characters, and we refused to name them evil.

As we prepare to enter the bone cellar of the Night House, we get ready to encounter death stories, tales of darkness, devils, and sacrifice. We prepare to befriend not only our own shadows but also those housed within the world story, the beyond-human story we are all living right now. Remember the magick of the ancestral Red Hood, the medicine given you by the grandmothers and given *by* you to those old foremothers. Remember, you are healing the grandmothers just by breathing. Also recall the magick of the Coat of Moss, the way the Otherworld shapes, charms, and enchants your experience. Remember the feathery pelt, your wild skin that speaks to your shapeshifting nature, that requires a wild place to be seen. Last, recall the tattered hood, the foul and bright flowers, and that the naming of these shadow ghosts that haunt allows you to reclaim their power.

Wear these wild skins well as you enter the bone cellar. Notice how your world is changing, how your own story shifts along the gradient of these fairy tales. When you feel ready, as a final symbolic action, complete your work with the first level of the Night House by finding a threshold. As before, this threshold might be a natural boundary of some sort, a small creek or tree line, or it might be a built threshold like a doorway or a gate. Whatever your threshold, cross it mindfully, speaking a small prayer that begins like this: *I have worn the tattered hood, and now I know...*

We move now into the bowels of the Night House, into its bone cellar. Here we surely become rendered by the tales that follow. A good story wants the dark, after all.

Lessons from the Hidden Rooms and Wild Skins

You are healing the wounds of your grandmothers just by breathing.

The Otherworld participates in our everyday experience.

There is a time and a place to wear the wild skin.

Name the ghosts that haunt you, and their power becomes yours.

Part II

The Bone
Cellar

Chapter 5

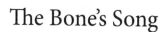

The Bone's Song

We all begin as a bundle of bones lost somewhere in a desert,
a dismantled skeleton that lies under the sand.
It is our work to recover the parts.

Clarissa Pinkola Estés, *Women Who Run with the Wolves*

There are places inside us where we dare not look, treacherous psychic grounds we have no map for, hidden corners buried deeper than bone. Fairy tales have a way of shining a soft light into these dark realms; there unnamed bogeymen, night-dwellers, and devils blink and shield their eyes from our lanterns. There we hear the bones singing, and we listen intently for words we may never have heard, for the secrets we might not have learned had we not met that fateful once-upon-a-time tale.

In the depth of the Night House, we find ourselves alone with the bones' voices, and they will not be ignored. No matter how deeply they're buried, no matter the fires that charred them or the cities that rose and fell overtop them, the bones remain. Their song endures, and now we can't help but listen.

Bone stories are underworld stories; they speak to death, yes, but also to ancestral wisdoms, initiation, and the necessity of periodic descent. Who would we be without our most initiatory experiences? We are sculpted by our initiations, made slowly and surely more whole by them, these parts of our lives where we are marked by the severance, the peculiar liminality that follows the death-of-the-old, and the final renewal where we become someone different, where we claw our way up from the soil, spitting pomegranate seeds and howling our soul-song.

In the bone cellar of the Night House, we turn our attention to the middle phase of initiation, our metamorphosis in the dark underworld cocoon. Here the threshold has been crossed. The severance from the old way of being has happened, but the rebirth has not yet come. We are a puddle of imaginal cells, Inanna suspended on her shadow sister's hook, a faceless traveler in Persephone's deep winter lands. Here we have no choice but to be rendered by our own becoming. We let death sit next to birth, and we welcome the ghosts that know us best.

Invitations for Tale-Tending:
A Personal Narrative of Initiations

We find ourselves in an underground room now, and the walls are lined with the bones of who we once were. We hear the bones' rough hum. We listen, and we consider our many initiations.

When have you experienced the death-of-the-old in a way so profound it sent you straight to the underworld? Upon emerging, you can clearly see you emerged as someone new. Initiations might be chosen, or they might be put upon you; many are somehow both. They might be bitter, even poisonous. Few are sweet. Without reliving any of the more difficult chapters in your life, allow a few of these death-void-birth stories to step forward and be witnessed by your wiser self.

Often, when we reflect on our initiatory chapters, we find a discernible narrative that is akin to our soul's story in this life. You could script the outline of your memoir by considering those death-void-births. In our story, the girl does not choose her initiation, her death. She does not choose it, but it comes for her just the same, and her bones cannot help but sing the story even after she's gone. This gnarly tale illuminates our first lesson from the bone cellar: Our stories will outlive us.

Our stories will outlive us.

Call to mind the mythic image of the singing bone. How do you see and hear it? What does its song sound like? What season is it? What hour of the day? Where and how do you encounter this image of the bone that sings? How does it make you feel? In your journal, write or draw a description of the singing bone. Ask, If the singing bone speaks to me now, what is it saying? Write this down, your message from the bone that sings.

STORY ALTAR: THE TALES THAT REMAIN

In working with this dark story, build an altar to give it a place to live. As before, this symbolic action shows respect to the story, but for these sorts of stories, the altar serves another vital purpose. If the story has a physical place, you can let it take root there rather than inside your mind. A story can be like an unwanted guest in your psychic house, and we want to meet this story, sit with it for a time, and let it go. The altar gives the story a boundary, a well-kept guest room so you can locate it, so it doesn't haunt your halls.

On your altar to the singing bone, place objects that remind you of the stories that live in your own bones. The stories that remain, the witnessed and the unwitnessed. The objects do not need to have any meaning to anyone other than you. Maybe a crystal represents a spiritual awakening you had in your twenties. Maybe a deer bone represents the death of a friend. Build this altar, allowing the stories of your life to come forward. Take care, and listen for the quiet songs that seem to come from nowhere.

The Bone's Song

Once in a time that is forever gone and come again, a king lay dying. The queen knew it was time to choose who would be the new leader, her son or her daughter, for the land could not be without a ruler, but she loved her children equally and could not decide. At her husband's deathbed, she prayed for divine direction as the king took his last breaths.

While a spring storm raged, the king passed to the Otherworld. That very night, the queen was graced by a telling dream, and when she woke, she knew what to do.

"In these wilds that surround the castle grows a golden flower," the queen told her children. "A flower so rare few have ever laid eyes upon it. Whoever finds this flower will be crowned."

The prince wanted desperately to be king, and he set out immediately to find the flower. The princess had no desire to rule, so she took her time, wandering the woods slowly and not straying far from her home. Three days passed while the children walked the forest, while the prince kept his eyes on the ground, refusing to rest, full of faith he was the chosen one.

The princess spent those three days eating the berries she knew were good, drinking from the clear-running stream, and sleeping at the mossy roots of the great oak trees. On the third morning, she woke just before dawn to the sound of mourning doves. A strange feeling stirred in her heart, but she could not name it. The forest was full of fog and dew, shining in the last of the silver moonlight, and just as the sun began to rise, she saw it.

A brilliant gleam stunned her eyes, and a lone golden flower unfurled its petals in the distance. The princess stood, took a breath, walked to the flower, and plucked it from the earth.

"I am to be queen," she whispered, afraid, surprised, and unexpectedly thrilled. She started home, dreaming of how she might heal the wounds of the world. For hours and hours she walked, growing tired and deciding to rest as dusk fell.

"Keep going," the wind howled through the trees, but her eyes were heavy. She curled up to sleep just off the road near a fairy pool, clutching the golden flower to her heart.

As night fell and the new moon rose high in the sky, the discouraged prince, unable to find the flower, was heading home. He might have missed her, but just as he was passing her the breeze bent the trees just so, and the moonlight flashed on the golden flower. Full of envy and ire, the prince stood above his sleeping sister.

So easily could he take the flower from her hands. He would be home and named king before she woke, but then she would tell their mother the truth of things.

I have no choice, the prince thought, and he pulled his blade from its sheath. Without apology, he took the flower and cut his sister's throat. Though she couldn't speak her last words, she stared her brother in the eye while her life faded. He cut her into pieces and buried her hastily, her head and torso tucked into the hollow of a dead willow, her legs under a heap of pine needles, and her arms left under the leaves right there near the fairy pool. Later that same day, he was crowned king.

Three years passed while the new king ruled the kingdom poorly. He enjoyed the privileges of his position and took on none of the burdens while the queen-mother mourned her missing daughter, who never returned.

On the third anniversary of the princess's death, a shepherd was searching for one of his lost sheep when he happened upon the fairy pool. The water was blood-red, and as soon as he saw it, the wind in the forest died. The birds quieted, and the shepherd held still. Suddenly, a soft hum seemed to come from the ground, and he saw a bright ivory stone in the dirt.

He knelt to pick it up, digging into the ground with his hands, but found it was no stone. He pulled one of the princess's arm bones from the ground, thinking it belonged to an animal. As soon as it was unearthed, the fairy pool cleared as if blood had never tainted its water.

"This bone will make a fine flute," the shepherd said, beginning to carve at it slowly and with great care. "I'll use it to call my lost sheep home."

When it was ready, he blew into the bone, anticipating a splendid sound, but to his great shock, a voice emanated from his instrument.

"We sought the golden flower, my brother and I," the voice crooned, and the whole story poured as a song from the end of the bone. "I have died. The king has lied," the song ended, and the weeping shepherd blew with his breath into the bone again, starting the song all over.

Each time, the song was the same, and the shepherd knew it must be shared. He began traveling, playing the flute on every street corner and in every ale house. All who heard the sorrowful song wept for hours, lamenting the pain of the world, for the voice was so pure and full of melancholy.

One fateful evening, one of the queen's knights heard the bone's song, and he recognized the voice of the princess. He offered the shepherd a great fortune for the bone, telling him he knew the mother of the girl to whom the bone belonged, and the shepherd refused to take any payment.

"Let her mother hear this story so she knows the truth of things," the shepherd said, and the knight brought the bone to the queen and played the song all night long for her while she wept, while she learned what her son had done, while she grieved for her daughter.

"He is no king," the queen said the next morning, and she played the bone's song for the entire kingdom to hear. No one who heard the song could refute the story, and the king was cast out of the land forever. The queen crowned the knight who brought the bone to her as the new king, and the princess's body was recovered and buried with great ceremony.

And the story ended, only to begin again.

The Three Rites of the Singing Bone

The story of the singing bone speaks to the soul's endurance. In our tale the story of the girl's death lives on after her last breath. The story itself seeks justice, and the bone keeps singing and singing until the wrong is made right. Of course, we know it cannot be made truly right since the girl is gone.

Now that our tale has ended, what do you still wonder? In your journal, name your question about the missing pieces of the story, what still seems egregiously unfair or imbalanced. This story, like many of our bone cellar stories, often causes a visceral reaction. Try to hold the tension of whatever rage or upset steps forward, and name your question.

After you have named the question, it might feel best to let the story brew for a bit, to let the question sit. When you feel ready, though, ask yourself this: What's underneath that? What wisdom is housed inside that question? Why is that the very question of my life right now? Script a new question that feels like a personal query, even a secret question you would never share with anyone. Write this new question down. We'll call this the singing bone's question.

If you look now at your message from the singing bone, the message given you by the image of the bone that sings before our story began, how is that lesson an answer to your new question? What do you notice when you examine this question-and-answer pairing? Stay curious, and see what you can see. Let this be your place to begin, your orientation as you start the Three Rites of the Singing Bone.

Rite I: The Kingdom's Renewal

Particularly with difficult tales where death comes to the innocent, remember to frame all characters as aspects of your own psyche, of forces that operate in our world, or of both. It is potentially hazardous to overidentify with the princess, to take on the whole of her story without reflecting on the part of your psyche that is also the king, the queen, the brother, the shepherd, and the knight.

At the beginning of our story, the king has died. In the old stories, when the king is ailing and near death, we know the kingdom is about to undergo a great transformation, a rebirth that, like birth itself, is not without peril. Kings and queens in stories mirror the forces of sovereignty, for better or worse. When the old king dies, we can wield a narrative intelligence and understand that this indicates our old inner ruler giving way to a new sovereignty.

For our first Rite of the Singing Bone, reflect briefly on the rules you have set up for yourself that no longer make sense, the boundaries you erected to keep your path clear, to remain certain and, of course, to stay safe in dangerous places. You might focus on a single life area, such as your work, spiritual path, health, money, home, or relationships; consider which of these life areas feels most transitional now and ask, What rules must I break to midwife this transition? What old rules must take their last breath and fall away? These rules used to make sense, used to resource you, but now you sense they are broken, outmoded, and on their deathbed.

Choose one of these "deathbed rules," and write a brief eulogy. Begin with these words: *Here lies the old king, the old rule that…* You might say, for instance, *Here lies the old king, the old rule that I must never take risks in my work or the old rule that to be without a partner is to be lonely.* Continue your eulogy by naming how this rule limits you, how you are ready for it to fall away, to invite the renewal of your kingdom, but also be sure to offer gratitude to this old rule for protecting you, supporting you, or whatever benefit it may have yielded, once upon a time.

After you have written this eulogy, go to a place you might call holy, read your words aloud, and safely burn the page, watching the smoke rise, sensing the air of liberation. Hold the tension of grief, of a certain ache in the heart that speaks to the ritual's importance, and, if you can ethically do so, leave a stone, a symbol carved in the dirt, or other marker there in that hallowed place before you go.

Rite II: Protecting the Golden Treasure

In our story, it is the princess who finds the shining flower, the golden treasure that her mother requested. We can think of the princess and prince in the story as the maturing inner authority, innocent rulers whose wisdom is not yet fully realized and therefore unstable and unpredictable. Consider the plight of very young celebrities, the child royals, and adolescents who are in the public eye; while most of us are able to test the boundaries of what it means to be civilized during this time in our lives without having every mistake illuminated, the very young and very famous have millions of witnesses to their maturation. We watch them succeed and fail. We see their shining gifts and, sometimes, their bleeding wounds.

In our story, the prince and princess are sent into the wild woodland to find their treasure, the gift that will open the next great possibilities in their lives, a metaphor for the adolescent rite of passage. Off they go to face death, to encounter threats to whom they believe themselves to be, and if they survive, to uncover a new name. Once the treasure is found, however, it must be protected, kept safe from the beasts lurking in the wilderness.

After the princess finds the flower, she falls asleep. In her innocence, she cannot see the dangers she faces now that she possesses the golden, growing treasure. Innocent eyes see no merit in vigilance, and the princess has no reason to believe her brother will kill her for the flower she found. This treasure, the shining gift, requires wisdom, discernment, and knowing care, but neither the prince nor the princess, as the less mature ruler archetypes, yet possess the character traits of a wise king or queen.

For our second rite, again consider the great and wild gifts you came into this world with, your own shining treasures. Look to the moments in your life when your creativity was witnessed, when your gift was made visible. Look to the actions, the art, that make you feel the most you, that make linear time fall apart. When you feel ready, find an object that speaks beauty to you, a symbol of your shining gift, the golden flower in our story. This might be a crystal, a stone, or even something you made with your own hands. Let it be something that will endure rather than something fragile that might dry, crumble, or get lost.

When you have this object, bundle it with care. Wrap it in fabric or build a small nest for it. Bind it with ribbon and maybe a few strands of your hair. Bless it with your spit and tuck it away. Place it somewhere secret where it cannot be stolen. Invite your ancestors to guard it when you cannot keep it safe. Let this be a symbolic action of respecting your gifts enough to protect them, to see their value and shield them from those who might misuse, manipulate, or even destroy them. Speak a final prayer over your bundle, and return to bless it from time to time.

Rite III: The Shepherd Meets the Warrior

At the end of the story, it is the shepherd who uncovers the bone, who hears it sing its story for the first time. The shepherd is the inner caregiver, the nurturer, the part of you that is fed by caring not only for others but also for yourself. It is an empathic act, unburying the bone and allowing the song to come through, the story to be heard. Only the caring one, only the one who steps softly, who seeks the sheep, another symbol of innocence, is able to find the bone and hear it sing, but it is the knight, the warrior, who brings the bone to the queen.

Embodied in the knight, we have another powerful archetype, our inner warrior who boldly faces challenge, who does so with great skill, who upholds justice and truth. It is the knight who creates the conditions by which the song can be witnessed by the queen, by the wise ruler. To simplify this small plot, we could say that it is our inner nurturer who uncovers the story of the wound, who does so as an act of care, and gifts this story to our inner warrior, the part of us that wields the courage necessary to carry the story to the ruler who will adjust our inner authority accordingly, who will make the wrongs right.

Consider these three archetypes, these living, energetic bubbles of meaning, as they operate in your story. What does your inner nurturer do for you? What feeds this nurturer, and when do they thrive? What stories have they brought out of the dark and into the light as acts of self-care? When have they held a difficult story long enough, nurtured it with loving warmth, before giving it to your inner warrior, the one who will fight for the truth and make it known?

Approach this final rite with great care, as the shepherd would. Check in with your inner wise one, and see if now is the right time to move through this healing process. If the answer is yes, if now is the time, go into nature, if you are able. Find a place where you can be alone near running water. If you play a musical instrument, bring it with you.

Begin by inviting your loving protectors, your guides, your ancestors, and any otherworldly helpers to come close, to bear witness to this ritual, to resource you in this moment. Begin to make soft sounds now, with your voice, with an instrument you brought, or by drumming lightly on your thighs or with your breath. Let it just be sound to begin. As you do this, imagine it is your inner nurturer who allows this song to be heard. The song is healing. The song is care.

If lyrics or chants want to come through, let them, but do not force the words to come. Your bone's song might simply be sound. Keep going. This is a song, a sound story, that your inner shepherd is bringing through today. It might be a wound song, a scar song, a heart song. You might know of the song's origin or nature. Let it come through just the same, and imagine the running water carrying it away to a place of greater truth. Stay with this for as long as you can, and when it feels finished, offer a prayer of gratitude to the wild unseen ones who stayed there with you, to your inner nurturer who shepherded the song out of the dark and into the light.

The Missing Ones and the Warrior Birds

In reflecting on this story, as with many others, we want to scream that it is not fair. Though the truth is finally heard, though the secret does not stay buried, the princess remains dead. Our fury over the missing ones, over the lost women who are never found, the indigenous women never searched for due to white supremacist systems, the little girls who never come home after school, is righteous and writhing ire, and it is fully and wholly justified.

There is a story similar to "The Singing Bone," the tale of "The Woman with Hair of Gold," where a maiden is killed and buried in secret, and her blonde hair grows up through the ground like hollow reeds. The shepherds used these reeds to make flutes, and the flutes would sing the song of her terrible death. Clarissa Pinkola Estés recounts this story, saying, "part of the miracle of the wild psyche is that no matter how badly a woman is 'killed,' no matter how injured, her psychic life continues, and it rises above ground where in soulful circumstances it will sing its way up and out again. Then wrongful harm done is consciously apprehended and the psyche begins restoration." Within the confines of our story, between the once and the after, the princess is not resurrected but, within us, within those who meet this story in wonder, the innocent is liberated and the secret is freed from its cold, dark underground.

In our next story, we encounter the warrior bird-woman, the one who will not sit idly by while women go missing. Remember your bone's song as you go forward. Remember to tend to the shepherd's search, and notice how nature organizes itself around you as you do this work. When you feel ready, move through another threshold crossing to signify your transition. As before, find a built or natural boundary, name it holy, and cross it with care. After you've done so, freely speak a prayer that begins with these words: *I have heard the bone's song, and now I know...*

Ready yourself now to meet our fiercest creature yet, our warrior bird-woman who leads her sisters into battle, a battle for the feminine soul where the old magick is afoot. Recall your experiences with the Rites of the Singing Bone, with the dreams that followed and the weather that shaped these rites for you. Into the mage's mansion we go, with feathered wings spread wide.

Chapter 6

The Mage's Bird

In a sense, we are servants in this life, each having come to life in order to serve something greater than our little-selves. No matter what costume we may wear or what status we may achieve, we are all on the way to the dark inn or the old cave where the dark angel calls to us.

MICHAEL MEADE, *Fate and Destiny*

Part of our work in these troubled times, if not our only work, is to tend our unique purpose. This means that no matter the horror, no matter the news stories of ecocide and genocide, no matter the grip of politicians' hands on our bodily autonomy, no matter the brutality of war, we are tasked with tending to our purpose as much as we are able. That purpose includes truth-seeking and truth-telling.

To ignore the world's shadow is to shun our own monsters, to keep our own shadows locked in their psychic prisons, where they can do the most harm, so our sacred work demands we look in the difficult places. We must see the atrocities, past and present. We must not look away, but neither can we be frozen in our witnessing. We can, and indeed must, see the blood and keep going. We weave our rage and our anguish into our art, whatever that art might be, and we keep our wild skins close.

All of us are here and now for a reason. We are born to do one quite specific thing, to pursue a singular purpose. If we pay attention, if we are permitted the time required to pay attention, we can see the emergent themes in our lives that illuminate this unique role we play in the world story, the role we play no matter the weather. Even as the fires rage and the waters rise, we remain bound to purpose, the "object to be kept in view."

Our second story from the bone cellar speaks to one woman's role, one woman's purpose, in seeking justice for the lost women. She, this warrior bird, is tasked with acting with great discernment, stitching together her dismembered sisters, protecting innocence, and setting her world right so the predator cannot rise again. Throughout her work, the warrior bird is cunning and calculating. She stays a step ahead of the monster, able to defeat him only because she understands she cannot lose sight of her purpose, no matter the horrors she witnesses behind the red door. She cannot get blood on the egg. She cannot, even as her world falls down, jeopardize the integrity of her creative innocence.

Invitations for Tale-Tending:
The Infinite Potential of the Creatrix

We cross the threshold and smell blood here. This deeper place in the bone cellar is full of lost women, and we hear them whisper their names. We pray for them, and we rage for them.

In our story of the Mage's Bird are several potent symbols, mythic images that we intuitively understand even without yet knowing the whole tale. One of those images is the unmarked, pristine egg. Can you see it? This egg, like similar images in the old stories, represents the cosmic egg, the golden egg, the undistilled and infinite creative potential, the primordial womb from which all things are born.

The egg speaks to innocence, wonder, and birth, and the warrior bird-woman is able to navigate the perils that might kill her because she understands the value, the hidden meaning, of the egg. She knows the necessity of shielding the egg from the horrors that surround it. In the story of the Singing Bone, the princess fails to keep the treasure, and by extension her own life, safe and sound. In this story, the warrior bird-woman knows the profound importance of protecting the egg, even as she goes about her bloody business of setting the world right.

In preparation for meeting this next bone cellar story, call to mind the sensation that precedes the birth of whatever your primary art might be. This feeling is often akin to endless possibility, and it is not always pleasant. It is the pure-white page. It is the black cursor blinking on the blank screen, the open stage, and the empty cookpot. You feel an anxious anticipation, a jittery excitement in the body. The instinct might be to hurry and put that first mark on the page, to rush the project's identity toward its formation, or maybe to run away altogether. We are socialized to value the product over the process, the final shape over the shaping, but our next lesson in the Night House encourages us to hold the tension of the creative ache, to tend to the early stages of the art's gestation and protect it during its incubation. Here we consider this: Our creative innocence must be protected.

Our creative innocence must be protected.

If you call to mind the image of the whole, unhatched, and unmarked egg, what do you see? How do you imagine it? What sounds do you hear? When you hold the tension of the egg's image, how do you feel? In your journal, reflect on this image, and then ask, If this egg could speak to me now, what would it say? Write down this message from the wild egg.

Story Altar: The Mage's Basket

The medicine of this story comes through in strange ways. Because of the strong yet familiar imagery, you might start to see this story manifest in unlikely places. In preparation, as before, build this tale an altar-house so it can live there. On your altar, place a basket or a bowl that represents the "mage's basket," another powerful image in the story that undergoes a vital transformation. For now allow this vessel to symbolize a healing portal. In this basket, you might also place an egg, a symbol of your own potential, an unnameable force alive within you no matter the challenges of life. Feel free to also include bones and feathers, symbols of stability and freedom, respectively. You might also place a candle there, lighting it before you meet this story, speaking a small prayer over the flame to see what you must see, to know what you must know.

The Mage's Bird

Once in a time that came and went and is now here again, there lived three sisters. While all three women spoke the language of nature, the youngest sister truly understood the ways of the Otherworld; it had always been so, since the time of her birth. The wild ground they lived on had protected the three sisters their entire lives, as they were without parents, but a shadow had befallen the land in recent years.

At first the whispers of the missing women were few and far between, but they came swifter now.

"No one's seen the miller's daughter," someone would say. "She probably ran off," another would say.

A few moons would pass, and then the whispers would begin again: "You know the girl from the Smith farm didn't come home from the fields last week. No one knows where she's gone."

"Ah, well, she was always a mad one."

For every missing woman, there was someone who remembered she had done something strange once, and her disappearance was always attributed to unladylike behavior. No one looked for them. No one cared to know the truth, for the truth was far too terrible.

"We must be careful," the youngest sister told her older siblings, but they dismissed her.

One night, under a full June moon, the youngest sister had a terrible dream, a telling nightmare about a snake with a blue beard who swallowed her two sisters whole. When she woke the next morning, she knew the dream to be prophecy and took to her forest altar to pray. That very day, there was a knock on the sisters' door. The oldest sister, the one with the kindest heart, answered.

"Can you spare a bit of bread? I'm so very hungry," a blue-bearded beggar pleaded, holding out a tattered basket. The oldest sister took pity on the old man and brought him a freshly baked loaf, but as she placed it inside his basket, she was sucked inside, right along with her offering. He closed the lid and left before anyone else knew what had happened. Inside the basket, it was cold and dark. She begged to be let out, but it was many hours before the lid to the basket opened.

When she could see daylight again, she saw she was in the grandest house. Full of gold and silver, it was. She also saw the beggar had transformed into a finely dressed man with wicked eyes that matched the blue of his beard.

"You are under my spell now," he said. "I am the most powerful mage in the world, and I have chosen you."

"Chosen me for what?" the oldest sister asked.

"To be my bride, of course," the mage sniffed. "If you can pass my test, that is." He handed her a bright-white egg and a set of silver keys. "I will leave you here in my estate. You are welcome to go anywhere you like. These keys open every door in my house. The only forbidden room is the one in the cellar, the one with the red door. Do not, under penalty of death, open that door. Do you understand?"

She nodded, confused. "And…the egg?"

"Protect it. Keep it safe," he muttered, leaving the oldest sister alone. She spent the first few days of her solitude staring from the windows, willing someone to save her. When it was clear no one was coming, she went from room to room, opening the mage's many doors. Some rooms were gilded with gold and full of musical instruments. Others were empty and full of dust. When the night hours came creeping, she was sure she could hear women screaming in the silence.

By the time the moon was nearly full again, the oldest sister's mind was slipping into madness. She'd been inside every room now, every room except the forbidden one with the red door. Her thoughts were slowed by sleeplessness, and she couldn't remember how she came to be here in this grand house. She couldn't remember the mage's warning, and she'd forgotten her own name.

In her strange state, using the little key to open the red door was all that made sense, and she made her way to the cellar just as the brightest moon rose over the grand house. She clutched the egg like it was her guardian, whispered a prayer from her childhood, and held her breath. As soon as she clicked the key into the lock, she heard sounds of horror coming from inside the room. Suddenly, she remembered everything, and she tried to pull the key out of the lock.

"No, no, no!" she wailed, but the key was stuck. The harder she tugged on it, the more it began to turn, and before she knew it, the door swung open wide. The stale salt-and-iron reek of blood washed over her, and her eyes would be forever scarred by the sight that lay before her. The walls and floor of this blood-filled chamber were stained deep red, and a great stone well stood at the center of the room, severed arms, legs, and hair spilling out from it. The moonlight shone through a small corner window, bathing the death room in a terrible silver glow.

Some shadowy force pulled her inside the room. She wept, stepping slowly, and saw the well was full of bodies and blood. She recognized some of them — the silver bracelet around one of the wrists belonged to the missing miller's daughter, and she was sure the frozen-open brown eyes looking up at her belonged to the midwife who had disappeared last year. Unimaginably, she also saw the small face of the little orphan child who used to play in their garden.

How deep this insidious grave went she did not know, but she did know she had no choice but to run. In her frenzy, a drop of blood fell onto the egg, but she didn't notice. She locked the door behind her, tore up the stairs, and ran straight into the blue-bearded mage.

He looked at her, and then he looked at the egg.

"What have you done? You've left me no choice."

He pulled her down the stairs, took her into the bloody room, cut her into pieces, and tossed all of her into the well.

That very night, under the full moon, he returned to the sisters' house. Again, he was disguised as a beggar, and again he carried his basket. This time it was the middle sister who answered the door and obliged when he asked for bread. As before, when she placed the bread into his basket, she was sucked inside with the offering, finding herself alive but imprisoned inside the grand house. All happened as it did before, with the mage giving her the keys and the egg, warning her of the room with the red door and leaving her to her solitude.

Unlike the oldest sister, the middle sister wasted no time. Only a few hours passed before she began opening all the doors in the house, looking fervently for a way out and finding none. After only one day, there was just one key left to use. When she opened the red door, she saw everything her older sister had seen, but now she also saw her own sister's face in the well. Frantically, she tried to pull her out, staining the egg bloody, along with her dress and hair. She shrieked, she wailed, she howled, finally falling asleep right there beside the bloody well. When she woke, the mage was towering over her, his face full of rage, and this was the last thing she saw.

The next day, the mage returned to the sisters' house, and the youngest sister answered the door. Unlike the others, she saw through the beggar man's disguise. He reeked of blood, and she knew him to be a monster. Even so, she feigned sweetness and brought him the bread he asked for. As her sisters did before her, she was enchanted into the basket, but the youngest sister was ready for whatever might be coming for her.

When she emerged from the basket, she could sense her sisters' spirits trapped there in the grand house, and she vowed silently to set them free.

"Your sisters failed this test," said the blue-bearded mage, handing her the egg and the keys and warning her about the room with the red door.

As soon as he left, the youngest sister did something the others had not done; she took the egg and placed it safely inside a bowl in the kitchen. Without going into any of the other rooms, the youngest sister took straight to the cellar and opened the red door. She was prepared for the horror before her, for she had dreamt of such things, but when she saw her sisters' faces twisted and frozen in terror at the top of the well, she clutched her heart.

"Strength," she whispered. "Give me strength." She heard the comforting whispers of women then, spectral voices encouraging her to keep going, and so she did. Slowly, surely, as the full moon rose, the youngest sister pulled her sisters' heads, torsos, and many limbs from the bloody well, laying them out on the ground until their bodies were arranged as they were in life.

"Live, live, live," the youngest sister chanted, and just as the moon shone a silver beam straight through the small window and into the dead sisters' eyes, they each took a breath and shot awake.

Disoriented and full of fear, they were, but the youngest sister explained her plan as they left the death room and locked the red door behind them. Eager to get revenge on the murderous mage, the older sisters hid in the kitchen as directed. The youngest sister retrieved the egg, unmarked and pristine.

When the mage returned, she presented the stainless egg to him, and he clapped his hands in delight.

"Oh! You have done so well! You are the only woman to have passed this test, and you shall be my bride!"

The youngest sister could sense that he no longer had any power over her, and she gave him an order: "Very well, I will be your bride, but it is only right that you bring gold and silver to my house. I will pack it for you, and while you are gone I will ready the house for our wedding."

The mage was thrilled and agreed. While he prepared for the journey, the youngest sister helped her older sisters into the same basket that brought them to the grand house, and then she topped the basket with silver and gold.

"This is quite heavy," the mage remarked. "How much gold is in here?"

"Less than I am worth," the youngest sister said, and the mage nodded.

As soon as he left, the youngest sister ran to the bloody room and fetched the head of the little orphan girl, the youngest victim, adorning it with jewels and flowers and placing it in the tower window overlooking the road.

The mage could barely walk half a mile without having to rest, with the weight of his basket burdening him so, but as soon as he sat down, the older sisters in the basket would call out to him: "There's no time to rest! Keep going!" The mage would look back to see the faraway face in the tower and think it was the youngest sister, his bride to be, telling him to hurry.

"You're right, my love! I'll keep going!"

This went on for many hours, the mage struggling to walk, taking a rest, and hearing the voices telling him to keep going. Meanwhile, the youngest sister sent wedding invitations to all the townspeople who had refused to look for the missing women, who had dismissed them as too poor, too strange, or too bold to find. Once the invitations were sent, she returned one last time to the death room and began the work of pulling the severed limbs and heads from the well.

One by one, she pieced the bodies back together and, as she did with her sisters, chanted over them, "Live, live, live!" Dozens of women took their first breath in a long, long while, and the youngest sister told them of her plan. The only body left in the death room belonged to the little girl whose head was adorning the tower, and they brought her tiny limbs to the kitchen to rest near the hearth, leaving the red door open so the dawn might cleanse the terrible space.

Just as the sun began to rise, the mage left the basket on the sisters' doorstep and headed home. The older sisters climbed from the basket as soon as the killer was out of sight, and they quickly went from house to house calling all willing women to join them in ridding the land of its monster forever.

Back at the grand house, the resurrected women helped the youngest sister cover herself in honey and feathers, and she bid them wait for her signal before taking to the road.

As she walked, she passed the wedding guests she had invited. She passed the old blacksmith who said the sheepherder's daughter "had it coming, whatever happened to her," and she passed the wealthy landlord who said the missing women weren't "worth the cost of a search party."

Each time, the guests asked her, "Are you the mage's bird? What is his young bride doing?"

Each time, the youngest sister would answer, "Yes, I'm the mage's bird. His bride is preparing for the ceremony, of course." She'd point to the tower where they could all see the face looking down on them, and they'd wave.

Finally, the youngest sister encountered the mage himself, and he said, "Are you my bird? What is my young bride doing?"

"Yes, I'm your bird," she smirked, pointing to the tower with a feathered finger. "Your bride is preparing for the ceremony, of course."

"Wonderful!" The mage hurried home, greeting some more guests along the way.

The youngest sister reached the trees of the haunted forest, and there she found her two sisters and a mass of women ready to purge their land of the predator forever. She waved a torch three times toward the grand house, and the resurrected women brought the head of the little girl to rejoin the rest of her body.

"Live, live, live!" they all chanted, and the babe took her first breath in a long while. Though all the others stayed, they sent the little girl away to the woods to hide. "You are safe now, child," the midwife said. "But don't come out until dawn. What's about to happen is not for your eyes."

Altogether then, the resurrected ones surrounded the grand house as darkness fell and the mage and his guests began to enter. The women stayed hidden but close and, so carefully, the women from the woods came creeping, led by their feathered warrior leader.

Just before moonrise, just before the mage and his guests could wonder where his bride was, the women locked every door, and every window, nailing them closed, and all together they set the grand house on fire. No one escaped, and it burned throughout the night.

By dawn the air smelled sweeter, and the grand house had fallen to smoke and ash. The warrior women returned home, and the youngest sister brought the little orphan girl home to live with her and her sisters.

And they lived well after, made so, as we all are, by gratitude and grief.

And so it is.

The Three Rites of the Warrior Bird

This is a telling tale for our time, a Bluebeardian story about the dangers of apathy, of refusing to see the shadows that lurk, and the necessity of protecting innocence. In the story the youngest who pieces her older sisters back together again understands she must enter the bloody chamber but also knows it is no place for innocence. While she in all her wisdom must go into the darkest place imaginable, she cannot allow the horrors she witnesses to stain the egg. Of course, that's only part of the story.

Now that the ever-after has come, what questions do you still hold in your heart? In your journal, name just one remaining question about the story. What seems to be missing? What do you want to know? Name this question, then amplify it. Make your question bigger. How is your question about the story also somehow, strangely, a question about the world? Maybe you asked why the older sisters did not listen to the youngest sister at the beginning of the story; this might become a question about why some women remain unheard even by other women. You might wonder how the mage came to be such a twisted man who preyed on women, and this question might become a query about cult leaders and ego-driven "gurus." Whatever your question about the story, let it become a question about the world.

This world question is your place to begin, your starting point before undertaking the Three Rites of the Warrior Bird. Recall now your message from the wild egg, the lesson you named from this image before our story began. How is that message a peculiar answer to your world question? Hold the tension of this question-and-answer pairing. Breathe deep, and begin the first rite, the Rite of Nesting the Wild Egg.

Rite I: Nesting the Wild Egg

While we have already named many powerful forces represented by the wild egg, the egg represents something else that we might call quite treacherous, especially during this arduous chapter in the world story. The wild egg is creative potential, infinite possibility, and also, therefore, hope. The wild egg is an uncracked house, a fragile dwelling in which some new, great, and unnamed yet-to-be stirs.

For our first simple rite, carry an egg to a hidden place. This might be an actual egg or a symbol of an egg. As you walk, for however long your journey is, consider this a symbolic action of tending your own wild hope. We live in a time when public despair, particularly as seen on social media, is far more compelling, even more seductive, than hope. It is far too easy to fiercely wail about what we do not want, to tear down those who seem to reflect this back to us, than it is to discern and name what we do want. The warrior bird-woman in our story burns the mage's house down but still protects the egg. She sends the predator and all who support him to their death, yes, but she shields the little girl from the horror.

Let this egg be a symbol of your enduring hope for the world, of your desire to protect innocence against all odds, and of the new, not yet named chapter in our world story. *Apocalypse* means "revelation" or "lifting the veil," and we sense we are in a time of revelation, when much of what was hidden is being brought to light. Allow the egg to represent to you the potential for the world to still be good, whatever *good* means to you. Let the impossible become possible. Leave your egg somewhere good, bless it with your spit and hair, surround it with wildflowers, stones, or shells. Let this be a small ceremony of tending the inhale before you speak the *once* in once-upon-a-time. This is your living ode to unmarred potentiality, to the hope that endures against all odds, even and especially now.

Rite II: Piecing Together the Lost Women

In other versions of the Bluebeard story, it is the youngest sister who is the most victimized, who is eventually saved by her older siblings. In our story, the youngest sister is the wisest, able to put her dead sisters back together again, to breathe life back into the lost women who would otherwise never have lived again. She then takes back the power of the mage's own basket, the very tool he used to abduct the women, and plans a careful attack. Importantly, while she alone protects the egg and defeats the mage at his own game, she does not go to battle on her own; instead, she gathers the women, those resurrected ones and those who feared for their lives.

Using the vessel you placed on your altar, or another of your choosing, consider the parts of you that have been lost and reclaimed over the years, throughout the many chapters of your story. Do not relive the most difficult times in your life. Simply bear witness to your experiences of reclamation. Reflect on what you might call your personal blueprint, your original soul map. What has been reclaimed during and following your many initiations? In addition to your symbol of the mage's basket, gather also some beads, coins, seeds, or something small. Have at least twenty of these objects for your ritual.

When you feel ready, begin to place the small pieces into the basket, one at a time. For each one, name something you have reclaimed, something that previously felt severed — by your hand or by someone else's — that now feels very present, very whole, and very healed. You might say "my identity" and place a bead in the basket or "my voice," "my story." Keep going until all the pieces are in the basket, then speak a prayer of gratitude over the vessel.

Rite III: Burning the Predator's House

The mage is a peculiar character. He represents the shadow side of the mage archetype, the sorcerer who seeks to manipulate, who uses magick to do so, and who is fed by wielding power over others. We see the shadow mage in our world frequently; they are the cult leader, the spiritual predator, the beast in the white robe. The mage in the story also walks the way the trickster walks, setting his own trap by making up the very game that would defeat him or render him powerless.

Trickster characters in stories are unpredictable. The trickster, like a fairy or *sidhe* in old Irish stories, might reward you greatly or kill you, and you won't know until you know. The trickster cannot be trusted, prefers to operate on the fringes, and like the mage in the story, sets their own trap. Once the youngest sister wins the mage's game, the game he set up himself, he has no power over her. Like Rumpelstiltskin, who dares the maiden to guess his name, the mage fully discloses his weakness and therefore sets himself up to be beaten.

The woman in our story does not just beat the mage at his own game; she also ensures that she is the last one ever to play that game. Unlike the Swan Maiden, who is a creaturely shapeshifter, who was born part bird, the youngest sister was made into the warrior bird-woman. The mage gives her the egg, and she hatches into the warrior that will defeat him forever.

For our third and final Rite of the Warrior Bird, gather a piece of paper, writing utensil, fire source, and burn bowl. When you feel ready, call your loving long-gone-still-here ancestors close. Invite your helpers, the loved ones in-spirit, any creatures you feel a kinship with, and all your unseen supporters. Call them close. Look for a sign that it is time; this might be the shape of a cloud, a sudden memory that steps forward, or a song that plays from a passing car; it can come from anywhere, but trust that you will know when it arrives.

When you have your sign, write on your piece of paper all you want to see gone from this world. Make a list of what you feel does not belong here. Think of the world you wish the children nine hundred years from now to be born to. What will they never see in this world of yours, and rightfully so? As you make your list, recall the egg from the first rite, tucked away and safe from this work you do now. Like the little girl at the tree's edge from the end of our story who does not see the burning, the wild egg is separate from this work.

When you are ready, begin to chant, "Be gone. Be gone. Be gone!" Keep chanting. Begin to read your list with the words "Be gone!" in between each thing you are banishing. Keep going. Tend to the rhythm of your heartbeat. After you've read the list, begin to hum gently, and rock from side to side. Set the list on fire, and watch it burn. Keep humming. The smoke rises. Keep rocking. The fire dies, the ashes cool. Breathe. Stay here for a time, if you can. Notice the visions that come. Scatter the cool ashes when you are ready, thank the ancestors and your other supporters, and return home.

Between the Lands of the Living and the Dead

Only in her warrior nature, only in wearing the guise of the warrior bird, was the youngest sister able to gather the women in their battle and see the story to its end. To wage war means to confuse, to befuddle. The type of war the youngest sister conjures is a dramatic one; she dresses up the little head of the orphan girl, knowing the mage will assume it is her in the tower, and she creates her own costume. Recall the associations between birds, women, and lewd behavior. Birds were associated with birth and reproduction but also the feathered bed, the marital nest. In the collected version of this story, the youngest sister rolls in honey, slices open a mattress, and then rolls in the feathers. She takes back the power not only of the basket but also the egg, as she "hatches" into something quite fearsome. She tricks the trickster into believing she is his bird and his wife, and then she puts an end to him.

Our inner warrior is the part of us that can reclaim the power of the tools that were originally used against us, but we mold these tools to best fit our hands. Sometimes we have to ask ourselves to name our power sources, to take stock of the instruments we hold that can trouble a system in just the right places. In our next bone cellar story, we meet the Girl of the Moon. One of her power sources — and certainly not the only one — is her ability to walk between the worlds of the living and dead; our power sources are not always socially acceptable, and nor should they be.

As you prepare to meet our next story, reflect on your work with the Three Rites of the Warrior Bird. Reflect on your power sources, the home of your vitality, and when you feel ready, find a threshold to cross. Mindfully and with great care, step across this threshold and speak a small prayer that begins with these words: *I have met the warrior bird, and now I know…*

Think of the wild egg, safe and sound. Think of the hope that endures even now, the ashes you scattered to the wind, and the times in your life when fearlessness found you. From here we step into the land of the dead.

Chapter 7

The Skull Groom

The English word "hell" comes from the land of the Scandinavian subterranean goddess Hel, but her underground was not a place of punishment. It was only the dark womb, symbolized by the cave, cauldron, pit, or well. The Dark Goddess was not feared and her abode was not a place of torture. She awaited her initiates in graveyards, the entrance to her temple. Through death, individuals entered the dark moon phase of their cycle; there they met the Dark Goddess, who led them through the intermediary passage back to birth.

Demetra George, *Mysteries of the Dark Moon*

To move between the worlds is to see or otherwise sense that an unseen intelligence is afoot, that hidden forces are affecting if not organizing our heavier, material experience. Some of these less visible energies participate in the human space, and others are completely ambivalent toward us, preferring not to be witnessed, dwelling entirely in shadow.

As young children, we do not question the Otherworld's existence; it simply *is*. The experiences we have as children that some may call supernatural are, to the child, quite natural and very present. There is nothing particularly *super* about them, at least not until an authority figure reacts to the child's description of the experience with concern. Our creaturely brains see by prioritizing the greatest threats in our environment, and because these forces — the ghosts, the land spirits, the loops in time, and other energetic forces too numerous and tradition specific to clearly name — are generally not a physical threat to our survival, we simply do not readily see them. Even so, they are there.

Fairy tales open the door to the Otherworld. While one can pursue many different practices to hone clairvoyance, clairaudience, and other psychic skills, an old story can serve as an effective bridge between the worlds. In the space between the once and the ever-after, our hard-edged beliefs about the natural and supernatural are challenged. Even the most closed-minded skeptic, if they truly listen to and meet a fairy tale well, considers that magick may be real as the tale unfolds. While after the story ends they might shun the notion that enchanted objects or shapeshifting vixens exist, they at least accept their validity while they listen. The story provides the container for the *what if*, and the imagination reaches into unexpected realms for which the listener has no map.

For this reason, among others, fairy tales trouble the overculture. Remember the connection between women-only spaces and storytelling. In *From the Beast to the Blonde*, Marina Warner asserts that certain women, these bird-women and spinsters, were socially denigrated in part because they "moved between the worlds," entering into spaces where male authority was not permitted. It was in those birthing rooms and summer kitchens where the tales were spun, and in those hidden places, limiting social conventions and misogynistic laws were not able to wield their heavy hands. This otherworld, in that way, possessed a liberatory quality despite the obvious role of class in necessitating these utilitarian, women-only spaces. The nobles did not spin their own yarn or cook their own meals, after all. These otherworlds were inhabited almost exclusively by lower-class women in positions of servitude.

In a birthing room, as in a fairy tale, life and death are simultaneously present; this is still true today, but it was even truer in centuries past. The light of possibility that a healthy baby is about to be born coexists with the creeping shadow of death, the very real threat that the mother, babe, or both will not leave the room alive. The midwives, the doulas, and the other women permitted inside the birthing room understood this well. They knew that a birthing room truly does exist between the worlds of life and death, hope and sorrow, joy and grief.

Our third story from the bone cellar is a between-the-worlds story, an old Nigerian tale of walking from the realm of the living to the land of the dead, and back again. Our heroine, our Girl of the Moon, learns about the value of otherworldly helpers and the dangers of spiritual seduction. Having lived beyond the veil for a time, she comes to understand the beauty of the living world, and she is all the wiser for it.

Invitations for Tale-Tending: Night Vision, Death, and the Dark Goddess

Soft moonlight shines through the window here in our next bone cellar room. We know ghosts are present. We sense the veil is thin. Here we are close to the Otherworld, and the Dark Goddess keeps watch.

Historically, fear of the Dark Goddess has been inextricably bound to fear of divination, seership, death, blood mysteries, childbirth, and the night. In our story the main character's name is Afiong, meaning Girl of the Moon. The moon has long been understood to share a kinship with the menstrual cycle, and this knowing crosses cultural and geographic lines. In *Mysteries of the Dark Moon*, Demetra George posits that partly because women often bleed on the dark moon, this end, this ever-after, of each lunation became entwined with Dark Goddess mythologies all over the world. Fear of the dark is inextricably bound to fear of death, the long sleep inside the eternal night, and while we have images now, many rooted in the Christian devil, of the masculine "grim reaper," in earlier centuries when plague was rampant and the healers were scarce, death was a woman.

In many old folk tales the spirit of a disease was depicted as female. In an old Irish folk tale collected from County Limerick, a man sees the spirit of yellow fever as a maiden in a yellow dress. He helps her to cross a river and then, understanding who she is, quickly moves his family to the opposite side of the river from where the plague spirit was traveling. Though many died, the man's family was spared. Similar stories exist throughout all parts of Europe, stories where disease was witnessed as a moving feminine entity.

Death walks beside us always. Death haunts our gratitude, as we understand that eventually, somehow and in some way, we will lose what we love. The bleeding body lives close to death. We feel and see our womb shedding blood each moon cycle. Some of us have had a pregnancy die inside our bodies. We know death is close, even in our greatest and most joyful moments, even when we are full of life.

Divination, seership, mediumship, and other psychic skills support our relationship to death. When we can see beyond the veil, when we walk with one foot in the Otherworld, we know that death is merely a portal, a door to another place. Many of us are socialized to ignore these skills when we are young, to let them atrophy in favor of social acceptance or religious norms, yet these skills can always be reawakened. It is never too late to improve our night vision.

In preparation for meeting the Girl of the Moon and her Skull Groom, take a brief inventory of your otherworldly moments. These are your ghost stories, your dreams that came true, your right-place-at-the-right-time moments. These moments are, to you, irrefutable proof that the Otherworld is an active participant in your life. Make a list of these moments, going back through all your many chapters. Name as many moments as you can, and then ask, What patterns do I see in these moments? Maybe many of them are specific to a place or a season. Maybe many happened at a specific time in your life, perhaps just before or just after an initiatory experience. What do you notice? Take stock and consider this, the next lesson from the Night House: Death is not the end.

Death is not the end.

Call to mind now the image of a nearly dark moon. Can you see it? Only a sliver of silver arcs along the left edge of this, our closest celestial body. What season does this dark moon seem to be in? How do you feel when you see it, and what lesson does this moon hold for you now? Write down a single message from the dark moon in preparation for our guiding story.

Story Altar: The Otherworldly Witness

The power, the charge of this story, may come through as feelings and sensations. Build an altar to this tale by including symbols of your psychic strengths, the ways you have been able to see in the dark. You might also include symbols of the otherworldly moments you listed. Let this be a space for the story to live for a time. Light a lone candle, speaking a prayer to your own beloved dead, those loved ones in-spirit you know still resource you from time to time, and ready yourself to meet the Girl of the Moon and her Skull Groom.

The Skull Groom

Once, never, and always, there lived a beautiful girl called Afiong, the Girl of the Moon. Men traveled from every land to look upon her, offering gifts if she would choose them for her husband. No man was good enough for her, she thought, and she always waved them away.

Little did she know that in the spirit world there was a skull, long dead and nameless, who watched her, always. The skull became consumed with desire, and in his wanting, plotted to disguise himself as a living man. He gathered the best parts from the men he knew in the spirit world, stitching a body together that would surely impress the Girl of the Moon.

When she saw him, he looked so stunningly beautiful that she agreed to marry him, and the skull took her away to the land of the dead. Her parents mourned her, knowing that no one ever returned from such a place, and as soon as the girl crossed the threshold between the living and the dead, the skull returned all his parts to their owners. He became only a nameless skull again, and Afiong lamented her choice.

The skull did not live alone but with his decrepit mother who needed much care, and the Girl of the Moon became a loving caretaker to the spirit hag. She tended to her day and night, and soon the skull's mother learned to love this strange human girl who somehow came to her house from the land of the living.

"We must get you out of here," the spirit hag said one day. "There are hungry ghosts here that will eat you if they learn you are alive. You are not safe here."

When the skull was away, his mother called the Spider to weave protections into the girl's hair that would keep her safe, and then she called the wind to come and carry Afiong home to the land of the living. At first a great storm came and was far too rough, not understanding Afiong's human needs, so the spirit hag called again, this time summoning a gentle breeze that carried the girl home.

Because she had lived in both worlds, the Girl of the Moon now saw all things more clearly, and she chose a living husband who was worthy of her.

They lived happily ever after, made so, as we all are, by gratitude and grief.

The Three Rites of the Spirit Hag

In this story we find a girl who accidentally moves between the worlds. Because her heart is good, because she helps the spirit hag who is essentially her mother-in-law, she is able to escape what would otherwise be a terrible fate. The spirit hag is her wilderness guide, and Afiong tends to her and her house even while she is afraid. We know Afiong is no ordinary girl. She is set apart from other maidens by her beauty, yes, but also by her ability to cross the forbidden boundary, not once but twice.

If you hold the tension of this story, what do you still wonder? In your journal, name a remaining question that nags at you, that feels strangely pressing. You might ask, What happened to the spirit hag? Or, Does the Skull Groom pull another girl into his world? Whatever you're wondering, write it down.

Ask then, as before, Why is this my question? You could have asked anything, and yet you asked this. Why? How is this the very question of your life now? Let the question itself be an oracle. What does it tell you? Reshape the question slightly to be a question about your life, about a transition you are moving through. Name this new question, this life question, and then look to your lesson from the dark moon image. What was the message from the moon you wrote down before our story began? How is this message an answer, albeit a strange one, to your life question? Allow this question-and-answer pairing to be your starting point, your first step as you begin the Three Rites of the Spirit Hag.

Rite I: The Wisdom of the Six Directions

What would it have been like to be raised in spaces where our other-worldly gifts were cultivated, celebrated, and amplified? The systems put in place by the overculture are often threatened by the seers, the mediums, the wise women, and the channelers. Historically this has been true. In *Caliban and the Witch*, Silvia Federici recounts the causal link between capitalism's rise and the European witch-hunts. It was not good for production, for instance, to have those well-versed in astrology state that it was not a favorable day for working. The influx of gold from the colonization of the Americas required the European economy to keep moving in order to manage the consequent inflation. Every day had to be a favorable day for working, and the denigration, criminalization, and eventual murder of those who threatened the emergent capitalist systems with their otherworldly knowledge seeded the seventeenth century witch-hunts.

The witch-wound runs deep, and reclaiming gifts that could once have led to suspicion, imprisonment, torture, and death is no easy task. In beginning or returning to such an endeavor, allow the natural world to resource you. This first rite is about the witch's ecological position and the availability of wild resourcing.

When you are ready, reflect on your otherworldly encounters, the list of your strange moments, experiences some might call unbelievable. Consider any patterns visible in these moments, and allow a certain orientation to take hold of you. If these peculiar encounters are showing you what might be a skill, a gift you have always possessed but are now being invited to hone, what is the nature of that skill? Perhaps you have encountered a ghost or two, and you wonder about your own skills as a medium. Perhaps you seem to just know about future events before they occur and you wonder about your claircognizance, your ability to simply know.

Hold the tension of this apparent orientation, and go into nature, if you are able. Find a place where you can be alone and, using a compass if you need to, face the North. Stand, breathe, and begin rocking your weight from side to side, from one foot to the other. Let your gaze go soft as you look long into the North. Wait. Invite a message from the North to come through. Let this be a message about comfort or validation, a sign you are going the right way. Trust you will know when it comes and, when it does, take note. Do the same with the East, South, and West. Notice the signs, the rumble of thunder or the mourning dove's keening. Stand with one foot in the Otherworld.

Get low then, and place your hands on the ground. Look to the earth and see what you can see. What sign do you receive from below your feet? Then, last, look to the sky. Lay on the ground if you are able, and look straight up until you receive your last, your sixth, sign.

You will likely not yet know how these six signs go together, but ponder this: What story do these six signs tell me? Let this be a lighthouse or North Star question, a question you move toward but do not quite answer, not definitively, not yet.

Rite II: Moon Scrying

Allow a few days to pass between completing the first and second rites. When you are ready, look to your experience with the six directions rite, and define a clear question about your otherworldly powers. It can be anything. You might wonder, for example, Where will I find my teacher? Or, How can I release this fear of seeing too much? Whatever your question, name it. Let it feel important.

On a night when you can clearly see the moon in the sky, find that silver beacon with your gaze. You can be inside or outside. Hold the tension of your question, and then move through these steps:

1. Keep your eyes fixed on the moon, but let your gaze go soft, easing your focus.

2. Breathe slowly and hum on the exhale to settle your nervous system.

3. Allow your inner narrator to speak, to complain, to tell you a story. Our inner narrator is always talking, but eventually, in a scrying exercise, they run out of things to say. Let them talk until the spaces between what they say get larger, larger, and, finally, all there is.

4. When your inner narrator gets quieter, you will begin to see what we sometimes call optical illusions. There will be two moons instead of one, or the aura around the moon will start to dance. What you see might be even weirder than this, but do not let these peculiar visuals make you sharpen your focus. Keep the gaze soft even as the strangeness takes over.

5. Imagine then that you are seeing not from human eyes but from your third eye. Imagine you are looking out a window that sits between and a bit above your brows. Your human eyes are fixed on the moon, but your mythic eyes see deeper. What do you see? Let the vision come. Let the vision come. Let it come.

6. Notice all you can about what you see, and then, when you are ready, return your attention to the moon.

7. Let your eyes close, and notice what you see behind the lids.

8. Offer a brief prayer of gratitude to the moon, and then open your eyes.

Write a reflection in your journal. What was your vision when you looked from the brow window? What does it tell you about your question?

Rite III: Time-Weaving in the Dark

Our final Rite of the Spirit Hag is a simple time-weaving spell for calling in what you desire. First, reflect on your work with the first two rites, and set a clear intention for this spell. Name a vision, a moment in the yet-to-come, that you desire with your whole body. This is a vision of you standing fully and wholly in your power. Perhaps you have brought a new skill to fruition, or you feel steadfast in your seership or your otherworldly gifts. Let the vision itself be healing. How do you feel in this yet-to-be moment? Name the feeling.

Now review your list of otherworldly encounters and find a memory that shares a similar feeling. The feeling will not be exactly the same. Often the memory's feeling seems to be a more diluted form of the vision's feeling, but the *theme* of the feeling is the same. For instance, if your vision is of you giving tarot readings to people and feeling fully sustained by this work, you might look for a memory of a time when your gift was witnessed, when you felt stable in your skill. Let the memory you choose feel like it resources you, holds you in the reality of your experience, giving you a firm ground to stand on.

Once you have the memory and the vision, find a place and a time where you can be unbothered. Invite your helpers and ancestors to come close. Invite the spirit of the six directions. When you are ready, face the direction that feels like home, the direction you associate with this vision you are calling in. Begin to shift your weight from side to side as you did in our first rite. Sense the power of the present moment.

Now begin to chant these words: "I am. I am. I am." Keep chanting, and call to mind your vision. See it. Learn from it. Amplify it. Make it clearer. The lines become sharper, and the colors become brighter. Keep chanting, and embody the feeling of this vision. Return to the present moment, but keep feeling the feeling with all that you are. Now call to mind your memory, and feel the feeling. Stay with this, a strange braiding of past, present, and future. Chant all the while, psychically dancing between the past, the present, and the future. Keep going.

You will begin to sense that linear time is falling apart. The memory will start to feel like the vision, and vice versa. This is your signal to slow the chant down, slow the rock in the body, and hold the tension of the vision one last time. Notice something new; it wasn't there before, but now here it is. Breathe.

When you are ready, hold a sense of gratitude in your body for the vision, the present moment, and the memory, and then become still and silent. Offer a brief prayer of gratitude to the directions and your many helpers and, importantly, look for your "cosmic nod." A spell is always followed by a sign from the Otherworld that tells you: Message received. It can be a creature, a dream, even an odd social media post that somehow shares something from your vision. Once you receive your nod, let the spell go.

To Charm the Yet-to-Be

Like many fairy tales, on its surface this wonder story is a warning not to want too much, to never dare disobey your parents or stray from the known road. On a deeper level, the tale is an initiation story of a maiden who travels, however unwittingly, where ordinary people do not belong. There she is kind to an old ghost of a woman who in turn becomes her savior.

Like the Greek goddess Persephone who dwells in the Underworld during the winter months but returns to bless the topside world with beauty every spring, our maiden Afiong returns to the world of the living stronger and wiser for having seen the world of the dead. The treacherous nature of stepping beyond the veil, of crossing the boundary that contains our heavy material world and entering the subtler space of spirit, is not something to be discounted. Yet we know that once any boundary has been crossed, it becomes easier to cross again and again because, essentially, now we have the map. Now we know the way.

The witch walks between the worlds, always. The witch knows the way, but that doesn't mean the way is always easy. Healing the wounds of the witch is a lifelong endeavor, but remember the first lesson of the Night House: You are healing the wounds of your grandmothers just by breathing.

As you prepare to meet our next tale, the story of the Ash Fool, recall your work with the Rites of the Spirit Hag. What did the directions, the moon, and your own shining spell show you about the next steps on your otherworldly path? When you are ready, cross a threshold, speaking your small prayer that begins: *I have met the spirit hag, and now I know...*

From here we begin to step fully into our power. We seek the old charms from the old stories. We listen to the trees speak, and we leave offerings on the graves of the foremothers.

Chapter 8

The Ash Fool

In fairy tales, as in life, punishment or fear of it
is only a limited deterrent to crime.

BRUNO BETTELHEIM, *The Uses of Enchantment*

I f we are fortunate, we will experience at least one initiation where we
are held by others, where we can sit in a circle with breathing, caring
souls and weep, where someone will feed us on a difficult night and put
us to bed. Many of our initiations happen in solitude, however. While
we know we are never truly alone, for our ancestors, guides, and even
our own wise-and-future self are always present, in some initiations we
feel quite removed from our relationships. Our people may not understand who we are becoming, or they fear they cannot resource us in the
way we need them to. No matter the reason, these solitary initiations
are often the most transformative.

In this story, our fourth story from the bone cellar, we meet the
Girl from the Ashes, our Cinderella. Forget what you know about her,
however, for this version of the story, the Ash Fool, is a tale too wild to
be a cartoon. Here we find lessons about good grief, learning from our
dreams, and slowly but surely becoming a force of nature that cannot
be contained. In part this tale speaks to the wise one's discipline and
dedication, and here we find inspiration for our own courageous and
purposeful transformation.

Invitations for Tale-Tending: The Creaturely Helper

Ashes cover the floor in this bone cellar chamber. The roots of hazel-wood trees grow through the ceiling, and everywhere are eyes that blink. We have all heard stories about the witch's familiars, the black cats, the wolves, the cunning foxes who help the witch move easily through the world, to stay less visible and remain hidden when needed. In our story our maiden finds magickal helpers in the form of birds and an enchanted tree; they not only listen when she weeps, but they solve her problems for her, grant wishes, and allow her to shapeshift into a form that lives closer to what she desires.

In preparation for our story, invite a creaturely helper to come forward. You might already know who they are. They might find you in a daydream. A telling memory might surface now, as you read these words, that shows you who your helper is. Whoever they are, ask yourself about the nature of this animal's power. What is its strength? How does it move through the world, and where does it dwell? How is the story of this creature like your story? Allow this helping animal spirit to come forward in your mind's eye now, to sit with you while you meet the next lesson from the Night House: The old stories contain powerful charms.

The old stories contain powerful charms.

When your helper is with you, envision them under, near, in, or even above a grand tree. See the wind blow through this tree's branches. Hear this tree's song. Hold the tension of this image, the image of the spirit tree. In what season does this tree find you? What does it tell you? Write down your message from the spirit tree. If it could speak to you, right now, right this moment, what would it say?

Story Altar: The Witch's Proof

In preparation for meeting the Ash Fool, give this story a place to live, to take up residence for a time. On your altar you might place some ashes, some feathers, and a twig or small branch from a tree. You may also include symbols of your "witch's proof." If you sift through your memory, can you find clear proof that your magick is real; these are the moments when your spells worked, when you consciously predicted a yet-to-be happening and your prediction came true. Whatever the nature of your magick, you have memories of your power. Take stock, and include at least one symbol of your witch's proof. Light a candle, and ready yourself to meet the Ash Fool.

The Ash Fool

In a time long, long gone and about to be, there lived a wild little girl who spoke the language of the trees. She knew well how to commune with the oaks under a full moon. She knew the secrets of every willow tree, and she understood well the mysteries of the grandmother sycamores. More than any other tree, though, she preferred the company of those prophetic hazelwood trees, and she sang their songs back to them. While she'd been born quite wise, as we all are, this little girl owed much of her otherworldly abilities to her mother.

An unruly woman, her mother had been called. A curse upon any man, the villagers whispered when the wild mother and child went into town. Nevertheless, the two were unbothered by the gossip and spent much of their time alone.

The little girl's father was often away, seeking a fortune that never came, forging bad bargains with devils and striking poor business dealings that left him deep in debt and deeper in regret. He hid his poverty well behind a reputable name and a grand estate house he inherited from his father, but he could never rest, never stay still, and the girl and her mother were left to tend the house all on their own.

He did love her, his wild woman, but as he grew older and his fortune grew smaller, he felt less worthy of her. He forgot who he used to be and why the world was good, and he left the fiery imaginings of his youth behind, along with his hopes of restoring his family home to its former glory.

Once a shining beacon of wealth, title, and grandeur, the House of Seven Hearths was falling slowly into ruin. From a distance, the stonework and arched windows were stunning in their artistry, but if you came close you'd see the tipping chimneys, cracked panes, and overgrown ivy. Even in summer, the house was always cold, and the West wind blew straight through every room.

Even so, the wild mother and child were at home here. All around the House of Seven Hearths grew great beauty, and they spent their days gathering nettles, berries, and dandelions. They spent their nights hearthside, sharing stories and building dreams.

As always happens, in time grief came to visit. One spring the wild mother fell ill. By summer, she was bedridden, and by the time the full Harvest Moon dawned in September, it was clear that she would never leave her bed.

No one had ever taught the little girl's father how to tend his grief, and he could no longer stand being in the house. He did not speak the language of death, and so he stayed away. The little girl was left alone to care for her dying mother and, just as the sun sank below the horizon one October night, her mother took her last breath, with her daughter curled up at her side.

The girl lay there for three days, not eating or drinking, until her father returned. They buried the wild mother without ceremony on the high hill behind the house, and every night thereafter, when the sun began to set, the little girl would go to her mother's grave to weep.

By the time the first snow fell, the father had taken a new wife. So deep was the little girl's grief, she scarcely noticed the new matriarch and two stepsisters at the dinner table. They didn't speak to her at first, the youngest among them, and she spent most of her time now on the high hill, speaking to her mother as if she were still alive, sleeping on the grave even as the nights grew cold and long.

It didn't begin that first winter after the mother's death, and it didn't begin during the second winter either, but by the third winter, the stepmother began asking the little girl to fetch water from the well, to mend the tears in the curtains, to make their beds, cook their food, and tend the many fires in the House of Seven Hearths.

The new women were used to luxury, you see. They were used to servants, silk dresses, and fine wine; none of that was to be found in the House of Seven Hearths, and in time they began to take out their frustrations on the little girl.

By her twelfth birthday, the little girl was spending her days waiting on her stepmother and stepsisters. She woke at dawn to light the seven fires and do their bidding, toiling until nighttime, when she'd smoor the hearths and go to her mother's grave to weep and sleep. This went on for years and years, the darkest time in the girl's life. Her father was almost always gone, and she was left alone with her tormentors. She forgot her old name, and because she spent so much time tending the fireplaces, she was often covered in ashes, and they called her the Ash Fool.

One night, on the anniversary of her mother's death, the Ash Fool fell asleep on the high hill as she often did, but on this night she had a dream. In the dream, she was full of ire. She was surrounded by seven raging bonfires, and she was howling into the ground: "I am the true daughter!" As she howled, a small tree began to grow from her breath, and soon there was a great green hazel tree standing at the center of the flames. Her fiery dreamscape stung her will alive, and when she woke, she felt changed. Something had stirred inside her, something that had been asleep.

She stood as the sun rose, pulled her filthy cap from her head and set her curls loose, and walked to the house with a boldness she'd never had. Her father was in the courtyard, readying his horse for another journey, and her stepmother and stepsisters were there, scowling in her direction.

"Now tell me, my daughters," her father said to the stepsisters. "What gift can I bring you that will give you joy?"

The Ash Fool stood next to her father, and the stepmother frowned, opening her mouth to give an order or send her away, but the oldest stepsister interrupted: "Bring me jewels, father! Jewels always bring me great joy."

"Very well," the father nodded.

"And me, father, bring me a silk dress, one I can wear to a grand affair," the youngest stepsister crooned.

"A silk gown it is," the father agreed, mounting his horse.

"Wait," the Ash Fool stated without emotion. "Do I not also

deserve a gift?" The stepmother and stepsisters gasped in shock. "Am I not the true daughter?" No one said a word, dumbfounded that the Ash Fool would use such a sharp tone with her father, and she continued. "On your way home, there will be a low branch from a hazel tree that knocks your hat right off your head." It was as if the Otherworld was speaking through her, and the others were afraid. The father, for the first time, saw his dead wife's spirit in his daughter's face. "Snap off a twig from that branch and bring it to me," she said last, leaving them all to their befuddlement.

Time moved strangely over the next few late-autumn weeks while the father was gone. The Ash Fool did many of her chores poorly and skipped some altogether. Instead of rationing the firewood for winter as she was meant to, she built seven raging fires in the hearths day after day, and the house was, for the first time since anyone could remember, too warm. The stepsisters feared and avoided her since hearing her true voice that morning, but the stepmother knew something had to be done. The Ash Fool was a threat to her and her daughters, and she needed to be put back in her place.

Meanwhile, the father, after years of failure, struck a lucrative business deal while he was away. On his journey home, he was lost in self-congratulatory thoughts. So distracted was he, he almost didn't notice when the hazel branch knocked his hat from his head, just as his daughter had said it would. He stopped, remembered her voice when she asked if she was the true daughter, and broke off a twig as he was told.

Upon his return to the House of Seven Hearths, his stepdaughters gushed over their jewels and dresses, oozing feigned gratitude, but when he handed the Ash Fool the hazel twig, she said nothing. She looked her father in the eye, nodded, and walked straight to the grave on the hill.

A thin layer of snow covered the ground, but the Ash Fool fell to her knees and dug and dug, clawing at the frozen ground with her bare hands and digging a shallow hole atop her mother's grave. She dropped the hazel twig into the dirt and returned the cold, stony earth and snow. As she did, ashes fell from her face, blessing the ground, and she whispered, "Shiver and shake, little tree. Silver and gold rain down upon me," and her whisper became a chant that became a howl: "Shiver and shake, little tree! Silver and gold rain down upon me!"

That night she fell asleep on the high hill but, for the first time since her mother died, she did not weep. Every night thereafter as winter turned to spring, the Ash Fool went to her mother's grave not to cry but to chant. Every night, she howled into the ground: "Shiver and shake, little tree! Silver and gold rain down upon me!"

By the spring equinox, a small sprout was growing up from the ground. By summer solstice, the longest day, that small sprout had become a grand tree, and by the full Blessing Moon in July, the tree had become the vision from her fiery dream, bright, billowing, and thriving.

Though she hadn't dreamt since that last telling dream, on the evening of this full moon, as she slept under the hazel tree's shadow, she dreamt of a grand ball where she danced with a wild king. In her dream she was dressed in a silver-and-gold gown embroidered with hazel leaves, the most beautiful dress she'd ever seen. In her dream she was full of joy, life, and purpose, as she remembered being when she was a wild child.

When she woke, she exhaled into the dawn, whispering her new name into the rising sun. No more was she the Ash Fool. This early hour, this quiet morning, she was reborn as Hazel. She pressed her hands into the ground near the tree's roots, remembered the glamour of her dream, and howled: "Shiver and shake, little tree! Silver and gold rain down upon me!" As she did, two golden sparrows landed on the low branch in the hazel tree, and she smiled for the first time in years.

Gritting her teeth, she returned to the house, where everyone seemed uncharacteristically giddy. An invitation had arrived that morning to the king's annual Harvest Feast, an event they had never been invited to before, and the whole family was encouraged to attend the three-day and three-night affair. The stepsisters were bickering about who would wear which dress, and the matriarch was mediating while the father reveled in this recognition.

Hazel tapped him on the shoulder, pulling him from his daydreams of even more prestigious invitations. When he looked at her now, he saw his dead wife in her eyes, and his heart nearly stopped.

"Am I not to go too, father?" Hazel asked sternly. "Am I not your one true daughter?"

He swallowed, and the others went quiet, listening.

"Yes," he said finally, his voice breaking under the weight of a long-gone sorrowful memory, and he left the four women there.

The stepmother was pensive and quiet, and the stepsisters returned to their preparations.

"We leave in one hour," the matriarch said finally. "If you can finish your chores by then, Ash Fool, I suppose you can come with us."

Hazel remembered her dream, the dance, the wild king, and the beauty of it all; she thought of this while she swept the hearths, brought the water, and emptied the chamber pots. She moved swiftly and surely, singular in her desire to attend the feast.

When the hour was up, she met her stepmother and stepsisters at the door. The stepsisters scrunched their noses at her, and the stepmother laughed, mocking her and saying, "Oh, all ready to go, are you? Just look at you!"

Hazel looked down at her ash-soiled dress and filthy hands. For the first time since she planted the tree, she felt that cold lump in her throat that told her she might cry, but she swallowed it, watching her stepmother and stepsisters leave.

Breathing deep, she went to the high hill, leaving a trail of ashes as she walked. When she reached her mother's grave, she pressed her lips against the hazel bark and whispered, "Shiver and shake, little tree! Silver and gold rain down upon me!"

Just then the hazel tree quivered with a summer wind, and Hazel was suddenly dressed in a stunning silver gown, silver shoes, and silver beads running through her long locks. Her hands and face were clean, and she was the woman from her dream, bright and shining.

A silver horse galloped up the hill, and she climbed on its back, arriving at the Harvest Feast just before dusk. As she crossed the threshold into the ballroom, all eyes were on her. Her stepmother and stepsisters did not recognize her, for she was so clean and full of life. She saw him then, the wild man from her dream, and they began to dance. Without words, the two of them moved to the rhythm of the old drums. For hours, they danced while the room watched and whispered.

"Who is she?" the strangers hissed. "How dare she keep the prince so busy! He's meant to be looking for a wife!"

When midnight came creeping, the prince finally asked her name, but she didn't know if he was worthy of knowing her yet.

"I must go," she said, pulling away.

"Wait." The prince stepped toward her. "Will you return tomorrow?"

She looked beyond the threshold to the full moon and said, "I will."

The silver horse brought her back to the high hill. She left the silver dress stretched out on her mother's grave with the silver beads arranged around the neck and the silver shoes below the hem, walking naked into the empty house. Her ash-covered rag of a dress was stretched out in front of the main hearth, and she put it on and went to sleep there in the ashes.

When she woke, for the first time in a long time, she did no chores. There was no one to order her to stoke the fire or fetch them food. As she did the day before, she went to the high hill and chanted into the bark: "Shiver and shake, little tree! Silver and gold rain down upon me!" And this time she was suddenly dressed in a gold gown that shone like the sun, with gold shoes and gold beads in her hair.

A golden horse came close, bowing low so she could mount, and she was swiftly carried to the second day of the Harvest Feast. As soon as she arrived, the prince brought her wine and bread, and she spent the day feasting and dancing, sharing stories of her mother with the prince and, of course, beginning to fall in love with this strange man.

Close to midnight, he again asked her name, and this time she told him, "I am Hazel."

"Will you return tomorrow, Hazel?" he asked, and she looked to the full moon.

"I will," she promised.

The golden horse carried her home, and she left the golden gown, beads, and shoes stretched out on her mother's grave, finding her own dress of ashes near the hearth and sleeping in soot.

When she woke, she took orders from no one except her own wild spirit, and she went to the high hill. Into the bark she chanted one last time: "Shiver and shake, little tree! Silver and gold rain down upon me!"

Suddenly, she was dressed in the silver-and-gold gown of her dreams with silver-and-gold shoes and silver-and-gold beads in her hair. A silver-and-gold horse came to carry her to the feast, and she spent the day in love with the only human who knew her real name.

At midnight, the festival was ending, and the prince begged her to stay.

"If you can find me, I'll marry you," Hazel said, rushing into the night so swiftly she left one of her shoes behind. He tried to follow her, the prince, but it was a cloudy night and the way was hidden as the silver-and-gold horse carried her home. All he had was her shoe, and he set his mind to finding his peculiar love.

All night he searched, but he was looking in the wrong direction.

As she had done the nights before, Hazel left the gown and beads on her mother's grave, but she brought the lone shoe into the house. She fell asleep inside the hearth, holding the shoe to her heart.

When she woke the next morning, the prince was there with his men, demanding to meet all the women who lived in the house and fitting them for the shoe she'd left behind. She watched while her oldest stepsister cut off her heel to fit into the shoe, and she watched while the prince rode with her up to the high hill. As soon as they reached the hazelwood tree, the two golden sparrows flew down and whispered into the prince's ear: "There's blood in the shoe. Look! Your true bride still waits for you."

The prince looked down at the oldest stepsister's white stockings and saw the blood creeping up from her foot. He called her a liar and brought her swiftly back home.

Hazel watched now as her other stepsister cut off her toes to fit into the shoe and, as before, the sparrows told the prince: "There's blood in the shoe. Look! Your true bride still waits for you."

When the prince returned again to the House of Seven Hearths, Hazel watched while her stepmother and stepsisters swore there was no other woman living there, and she watched when her father emerged from his grief and said, "I do have another daughter, my one true daughter."

Only then did Hazel step from the ashes and reveal herself, holding the other shoe. The prince barely recognized her, for she was dirty, but he asked, "Is that you, Hazel?"

"It's me," she said, and the two left together. As she rode past her mother's grave for the last time, the golden sparrows flew down from the tree and sang to the prince, "There's no blood in the shoe. Your true bride rides with you."

In time the wedding was set, and the wicked women received no invitation. While the stepmother understood she had been defeated and chose to remain home, the stepsisters dared to attend the grand affair, believing they would be forgiven and hoping they would be asked to live at the king's castle.

Each of the stepsisters stood on either side of the aisle while Hazel, dressed in silver and gold with a sparrow on either shoulder, walked slowly toward her wild prince. She did not look at the wicked sisters; they did not deserve her gaze, after all. As she passed them by, the sparrows flew from her shoulders and pecked out one of their eyes.

After the vows were spoken, the girl who dwelled in the ashes for so long, now soon to be queen, walked with her prince toward her new story. The sparrows flew from her shoulders, pecked the remaining eye from the wicked ones' faces, and took to the sky. The ghost of the good mother looked on while her daughter smiled, full of hope and life, sure to live happily ever after, made so, as we all are, by gratitude and grief.

The Three Rites of the Hazelwood

We all arrive at a point in our lives when we can no longer be what a younger version of us might have called *good*. In fairy tales, when the mother who is good dies, she often leaves children behind who must contend with her absence, whose lives are initially made worse because she is not there. Our story begins with this familiar loss of the good mother, and the little girl mourns her for years before she finds her own identity, her own power.

Now that the tale has ended and the ever-after has come, what do you still wonder? Name an aching question that can point you in the right direction. What feels like a missing piece of the story, some vital clue that would give the tale greater meaning for you? Ask this question now. Write it down.

Whatever the landscape of your life now, ask why that is your question. If the query itself is an oracle, why is that your wonder, the very question you need to ask about your life now? Reshape the question slightly to become more personal, to live closer to your heart. After you name this life question, look to your message from the spirit tree, the message the image gifted you before our story began. Let this message be an answer to your question, and let both the question and the answer show you what you need to see before you begin the Three Rites of the Hazelwood.

Rite I: Funeral for the Too-Good Self

An initiation begins with the death-of-the-old. Every initiation is also a severance, a leaving behind of the old way and the old name. If we frame this story through a personally relevant and narrative lens, we see that all characters are aspects of our own psyche. When the girl's mother dies in the story, this is akin to the death of the too-small, too-good self. Clarissa Pinkola Estés writes, "In the natural process of maturing, the too-good mother must become thinner and thinner, must dwindle away until we are left to care for ourselves in a new way."

As you begin the first Rite of the Hazelwood, consider when in your life you have let the too-good self die in order to allow a new power, a new sovereignty to be born. If you are over the age of thirty, you might look to the famed and feared Saturn return, when the planet Saturn returns for the first time to the place it was in your natal birth chart. For many this is a time of intense rebirth, generally occurring between the ages of twenty-five and thirty. The second Saturn return occurs during one's late fifties, another time of severance, metamorphosis, and emergence. During these times, a sacrifice is made, the sacred wound reopens and bleeds, and your old self does not make it out alive.

Choose one of these initiatory times now. Go to a place in nature where you are able to be alone for a while; this might be a woodland or a seaside, a mountain lake or an urban park. Wherever you go, look to the ground. Invite your loving helpers to come closer, speak a small prayer to the four directions, and then begin to freely speak a eulogy for the person you once were but are no longer, for the too-good self, the self that served as a sound parent for a time, provided protection and nurturance but had to give way to the wilder and wiser self. As you speak, begin to spontaneously arrange a small altar of natural objects; you might create a circle of stones, a small cairn from sea glass or shells, or a mandala of fallen leaves and twigs. You might draw in the river mud or place a flower petal for each memory or trait you associate with the too-good self.

Take your time here. Let there be spaces of silence where the birdsong resources you. Think of who you are now, how you have become the very teacher you needed when you were younger, and create an elemental ode to the good mother. Like little Hazel, kneel on the grave for a time. Tend to the spirit of your own initiation, and when it feels finished, offer prayers of gratitude to your ancestors, to your inner wild mother.

Rite II: Shiver and Shake

Sometimes, if we look, we find an effective witch's charm contained in the old stories. A charm in witchcraft must be spoken with care, must travel through time and space, gaining power the more frequently it is used. A charm cannot simply be written, left to wither on the page of a journal. A charm wants to live.

When the Ash Fool puts her hands on the dirt and speaks, "Shiver and shake, little tree! Silver and gold rain down upon me!" she is casting a spell with her tongue. She enchants the hazel tree to grow, and grow well. She calls in her most emphatic desires here and, by her will, it must be so.

In the old stories, silver and gold, when worn together, are the mark of the shapeshifter. We find silver and gold in many stories, of course, as these are quintessential riches sought by the wanderer, but here we have silver and gold together, in her chant, woven into her magickal garments and even coloring her enchanted horses that carry her to the festival. When you invite the image of silver and gold into your witchcraft, particularly into the visions you want to see made manifest, you invite a powerful mythic image that speaks to the treasured holiness of self, the inner wealth, and the gifts your soul came into the world with.

For our second rite, find a twig or small branch, perhaps one you had placed on your story altar, and let it represent the branch of the hazelwood tree from our story. In old stories the part represents the whole; a leaf can be the whole tree and indeed the World Tree, the ancient image we all somehow understand. A feather can be the whole bird or even all birds; a bone — like the singing bone — the whole story of a life. Find a twig that can represent the tree from our tale but also every enchanted tree from every old story, every mother tree that has ever brought comfort to a child.

Go to your garden, a wild place, or even a pot of soil. Invite the spirits of the North, East, South, and West to come close, to breathe power into this work. Begin to slowly bury this twig and, as you do, envision the fruition of a specific intention, a moment in the yet-to-come that you want to find you. With your human eyes, you see your hands digging in the dirt, but with your mythic eyes, you see this moment in the yet-to-come. Perhaps this is a vision of you having shapeshifted into a form that lives closer to what you desire, closer to your purpose. See it. Know it to be true, then amplify the vision by adding brilliant silver and gold.

Begin to chant now: "Shiver and shake, little tree! Silver and gold rain down upon me!" Keep chanting. Once the twig is fully buried, press your hands into the dirt and let your words become more powerful, louder and fuller. Envision this charm you speak traveling through time and space, to your own wise and future self and back through deep time. Keep seeing the gleam of the silver and gold in your vision, and stay with it until you receive a sign from nature that tells you it is finished. When it comes, when the crow squawks or the raindrops start falling, let your chant become a whisper and then go quiet. Breathe. Speak gratitude to the four directions, to those wild and unseen ones who resourced you, and last, envision a towering hazel tree growing right where you planted the twig. Like your vision, this tree also shines with silver and gold. Return here from time to time if you can, not to recast the spell but to see this shining vision of the enchanted tree.

Rite III: Wedding the Wild

Our final Rite of the Hazelwood is a soul wedding, a ceremony of intentional union. At the end of our story, as in many fairy tales, of course, there is a wedding. The wicked stepsisters attend, but they are not invited. The wild helpers, the little sparrows, blind the wicked ones so they can no longer see. The bride's new life will not be visible to them; they haven't earned the privilege of seeing her happiness.

Recall the Rites of the Moss and, in particular, the burning of the wicked ones' voices. In preparation for this final Rite of the Hazelwood, you might revisit that spell of banishment, burning to ash the written words spoken by the inner, limiting voices, those who want to keep you busy and small. In the Ash Fool story, the voices of the wicked stepsisters and stepmother want to keep her in the dust; they don't wish for her to ascend to their level, and she cannot if she's cleaning the hearth and mending their clothes. If you feel called, ceremonially burn a statement or two spoken by the inner wicked stepsisters, scattering the ashes as if they've fallen from the skin of the Ash Fool, watching the wind take them, then prepare to write new vows.

Reflect on the first two rites, the death of the too-good self and the vision-spell of silver and gold, and then, when it is time, begin to write thirteen vows. These are vows to wed your wise and wild self. There is an old Irish tradition whereon the first three wedding anniversaries the bride and groom decide whether they wish to stay married. Commit now to wedding the wilder self for just one year, revisiting this ceremony on the same day for the next three years, rescripting the vows, if needed. For now, ask, What are thirteen promises I can both make and keep to my own wise and future self?

You might let these vows be inspired by the four directions, writing three vows for the North, East, South, and West, sourcing the language from your own understanding of what these directions represent to you. Alternatively, you might look to your lineages, allowing the North to represent your mother's father's lineage. The East is your father's mother's lineage, and the South is your paternal grandfather's lineage. Last, the West is the motherline, your mother's mother's lineage. You might ask, What deep medicines run through these ancestral lines? If I go back far enough, what earth-based traditions are buried there that I am being called to remember, embody, and practice? Your final, thirteenth vow might be one that holds them all, a final affirmation of sovereignty.

Whatever your inspiration, write these vows now. Do not script any vows you know you will break. Shape your vows in a way that makes you feel powerful rather than anxious. Commit to nothing that feels too burdensome. You might say, for instance, "I will remember to see beauty in the rot" or "I vow to take care of myself when the day is hard." The vows can be anything, as long as they feel important to you.

When the vows are written, adorn yourself, if you like. Wear a veil to symbolize your incubation and emergence, then go to a wild place where you can speak these vows. Be witnessed by your ancestors, by the elements. Speak the vows aloud, facing the four directions in turn if you like, then recover a symbol of your ceremony. You might find a small stone or a leaf; if you can ethically do so, take it home to place on your altar.

Seal this rite in celebration. Go on your soul's honeymoon, if only for an hour. Do something that allows you to embody your thirteenth vow, your commitment to have and to hold your wilder soul from this day forward, in this life and on to the next.

Altars for the Dead

The Ash Fool is, of course, a Cinderella story, but we can see how the happily-ever-after was hard-won, arriving only after years of grief, rage, and healing. The blinding of the wicked stepsisters at the wedding is significant, as is the maiming of their feet beforehand. By the end of the story, the wicked ones cannot walk or see. Their ability to affect the servant-turned-sovereign's world is hindered, and only then does the ever-after come.

Reflect on your work with the Three Rites of the Hazelwood, from the grief ritual to the spell to the final wedding. Essentially, this is the plot of the Ash Fool, as she moves from innocence to wisdom, from loneliness to union. Consider the times in your life when you too moved from great loss to great gain, from the too-small life to one of beauty, one you might never have imagined for yourself, yet here you are. When you are ready, cross a threshold, speaking your small prayer that begins: *I have met the tree of silver and gold, and now I know…*

From here we prepare to meet our final story from the bone cellar, a story of wild innocence, of paying homage to the dead, and liberation from the cages that confine us. Here we find another plot in which the too-good mother dies, only to be replaced by a wicked one, but here, in this story of the Blackbird Boy, a great resurrection occurs. This is a story of honoring the ancestors, of telling their stories and giving gifts to the grave.

Chapter 9

The Blackbird Boy

*Grief has a sound, a sound that embarrasses the repressed
and offends the oppressive; grief is the sound of being alive.*

MARTÍN PRECHTEL, *The Smell of Rain on Dust*

The ability of an old story, a fate tale, to hold duality is irrefutable. In a single fairy tale, life walks with death, light with shadow, the civilized with the wild. The old stories remind us that life is better when death sits in the room, that we are made a little wiser each time sorrow finds us, that our encounters with grief ultimately amplify our joy. Every earth-based tradition honors the ancestors. The human animal understands we are here only for a time, but the ancestral story began before we were born and will continue long after we take our final breath.

In this, our last story from the bowels of the Night House, we find rituals of remembrance that sit alongside terror. We find prayers and altars to the beloved dead, and we find the wisdom of the innocents. Tending this tale means tending to the stories of your own loved ones in-spirit, the prayerful grannies and the outlaw friends, the nurturing matriarchs, dead kings, and the long-gone sisters. Allow this story to be an invitation to rekindle small ceremonies of honoring the ancestors and revering the larger, longer tale your soul joined but did not write alone. This once-upon-a-time happened before you were born, but you are no fringe character.

Invitations for Tale-Tending: The Ancestral Story

Framed pictures of the long-gone-still-here ones cover the walls here in our last bone cellar room. Before our story begins, consider the stories of your beloved dead. There you might witness hilarity and anger, respect and disdain. Whatever stories come forward, notice them, grant them a nod, and reflect on this question: What stories will be told of you? Of course you do not yet know, but hold the tension of the wonder. What role do you play in the ancestral story?

When doing ancestral work, it is crucial not to become stuck in the tales of recent generations, if you can. This work can present a challenge, as you do not know the names and tales of the long-gone-still-here ones, the ones who lived closest to the land. Although you don't intellectually know their legacy, here's the brilliance of this work: The stories of your ancestors are alive in you. You are the breathing, laughing, weeping ancestral altar.

> *The stories of your ancestors*
> *are alive in you.*

Envision now this image: A large crow sits on a low branch, eyes fixed on you. What else do you see here? What sounds do you hear? What does the air smell like? What time of year is it, and what hour of the day? Notice all you can, then write down your message from the crow. If this otherworldly corvid could speak to you today, what would it say?

STORY ALTAR: THE ANCESTRAL TREE

Before we meet the Blackbird Boy, if you do not already have an ancestral altar, build one now. Include small symbols of all four of your grandparental lineages, regardless of how much or how little you know about them. You might opt to represent the lineage itself, if need be, rather than any single person in-spirit. If you include pictures of your remembered dead, include only those you would like to speak to again, only those who are loving and would want to resource you. You might also include black feathers, small shiny beads, and other gifts for the crows, and a lone candle you light in the name of ancestral veneration, in the name of those who came before.

The Blackbird Boy

Once in a time full of sages and fools, there lived twin innocents who grieved their lost mother. These two wild children, a boy and a girl, dwelled deep in the forest and learned to speak the language of the owls, the hawks, and the crows. When their mother died, they buried her under an oak tree that had a great hollow in its trunk; there, each year on the anniversary of her death, the girl and boy left gifts in her honor. Seven years had now passed since their beloved matriarch took her last breath, and the oak tree's hollow was brimming with twig bundles, crystalline stones, and other treasures the children had found, prayed over, and left in their mother's memory.

No one had taught the twins' father how to grieve well, and the crack in his heart grew wider with every passing year. A poor woodcutter, the father struggled to feed his small family and thought it prudent to take on a new wife before winter came. In his haste, he married a jealous woman who despised children.

"You can barely feed the two of us," the stepmother would whisper after the children were asleep. "You must get rid of these hungry little brats if we are to survive the winter." Each night, the woodcutter's wife spit insults at him, berated him, and slowly but surely wore him down. It was decided that he would, on winter solstice, take the children deep into the forest and leave them there.

What the woodcutter and his wicked wife did not know was that the little girl had been listening to their plans and, on the shortest day of the year when their father led them into the belly of the woodland they had called home, she dropped small bits of ash and coal from the hearth as they walked. As they passed their mother's grave, a crow squawked loudly and spit a berry in the father's direction. The day waned, the full moon was rising, and the little girl was prepared.

"I'll...I'll be right back, my children," the woodcutter lied, his eyes wet with tears. "Wait right here." He left them near a small cave by the river, where he thought they would be safe for a time, where they would have water and shelter, but he had no plans to return.

Hours passed, night fell, and the girl thought it best to tell her brother what she had heard.

"So father's not coming back?" the little boy said.

"No," she answered sternly. "But don't worry. I have a plan."

The girl built a small fire, and they slept that night in the cave. In the morning the sun came late, but the two were warm and well. They drank from the river and started home, following the trail of ash and coal. When they passed their mother's grave, again a crow squawked in their direction. A warning, the little girl knew, but they kept going.

When the stepmother saw the two babes coming out of the woods, she was full of rage. The woodcutter was not home, and the wicked woman went mad with hunger and desperation. She took the axe from the wall, stormed from the house, and swung the axe at the children. The girl ducked out of the way, but the boy's head was severed.

"If you want to live," the stepmother snarled at the girl, "you'll make a stew out of your brother, and you'll say nothing to your father."

The girl spent the next long hours weeping and carving, praying over her twin's lost life. When her stepmother wasn't looking, she carefully took her brother's heart and brought it to the hollow of the oak tree.

"Bring him back, Mother," she whispered. "Bring him back."

That night, when the father returned, he was thrilled to see the pot of fresh stew on his usually empty table.

"Your daughter has returned," said the stepmother. "And she hunted some rabbit. Who knew she had such skill?"

"It doesn't taste like rabbit," the woodcutter whispered, sad for his son's absence, but he did not ask where he was.

That night the little girl gathered up all the bones from her brother's body and brought them to the hollow of the oak to rest with his heart.

"Bring him back, Mother," she prayed again, and fell asleep right there on the roots.

The next morning as a pale sun rose, the girl woke to see a fat crow with blue eyes staring down at her from a low branch.

"Is it you?" she asked.

"It's me," the crow said. "I'm safe now."

Full of joy at her brother's return, the girl skipped back to the house. The crow followed her, and the stepmother immediately recognized the bird as the boy.

"We ate you!" she screamed, throwing a stone at the crow in hopes of killing the boy's soul forever, but the stone turned in the air and hit the stepmother between the eyes.

She fell down dead, and the girl and her crow brother lived happily ever after, made so, as we all are, by gratitude and grief.

The Three Rites of the Blackbird

At the beginning of this story, we find the brother and sister in their grief. They honor their mother by leaving small gifts in the hollow of a tree. They keep her memory, and she continues to resource them even after her death. Like the Ash Fool's mother in our previous Night House tale, the children's mother supports their salvation but only through the participation of living hands. Only when the daughter brings her brother's heart and bones to the tree is he resurrected, and we know the spirit of the lost mother is afoot.

Now that the story is over, what small wonder do you still keep in your heart? Now that the ever-after has come, what question do you still have that feels pressing, that nips at you? Write this question down and name it oracle.

As before, ask why this is your question. What's underneath it? How is this question relevant to your life and, more specifically, to what life area does this question speak? Remold the question slightly now, reshaping the language so the question about the story is now specific to you.

Look to your message from the crow, the message from the image you wrote down before our story began. If you allow this message to be a strange answer to your question, what do you find? Draw no conclusions yet, but allow this question-and-answer pair to turn your head just so, to orient you in the direction you must walk now as you begin these, the Rites of the Blackbird.

Rite I: The Silent Supper

A traditional pagan ritual is the "dumb supper," a meal of silence that honors the dead. While the ritual is typically performed in late October or early November, it is powerful no matter the season. Who would you like to sit down and have a meal with again? Which of your loved ones in-spirit might like to take part in this ritual? You might name a blood ancestor, a friend, or someone else, but let them be someone you feel a strong kinship with. Let them be someone you knew, and indeed still know, quite well. Take care with yourself if you are in a state of acute grief, leaving this practice until you feel ready, until a greater healing has come.

Ask yourself now: What did they love? What was their favorite song and favorite meal? What colors did they surround themselves with?

When you are ready, prepare a feast at your table. Set a full place for your loved one, and prepare their favorite food. Serve them first, play their favorite songs, and most importantly, tell their stories. You can do this alone or with other living guests; if you do it with others, create a shared altar where everyone brings a picture or belonging of their loved one.

Notice what stories step forward and want to be told. Feel their presence and, when it is time, offer gratitude. Thank them for their lessons, for the laughter and the many memories. Bid them farewell, and leave their food outdoors, if you can, overnight. Look to your dreams for a transmission from them. Look to nature and the birds that fly. Know that death is but a portal and that their spirit lives on.

Rite II: Thanking the Mist-Spirit

In the old stories, as in our lives, we find many ancestral helpers. They are hidden and often unnamed protectors who keep us safe, who tell us not to walk down the dark alley or make that bargain with the devil. For the second rite, reflect on your story and see if you can sense a moment when you intuitively knew an ancestral protector was present. This might be a moment when you were in dire straits or in a moment of decision. Relive nothing through your body now. Simply consider a single moment when you sensed you were protected. You may have been aware of this spectral presence at the time as well; perhaps you were aware of some unseen hand lifting you from the water or a voice that whispered to you to keep going.

Whatever moment steps forward, trust that it is the right one. In the old story "The Handless Maiden" or "The Girl Without Hands," a mist-spirit follows the maiden as she walks the dark forest of initiation. The mist-spirit bends the branches so she can eat, dries the moat so she can cross, and keeps her safe while she faces her greatest and seemingly solitary darkness. Who was this mist-spirit for you?

You may not know the name of this unseen protector. You may still question whether they were there, but consider that maybe, just maybe, a loved one in-spirit walked near you in a time of great need. For this simple rite, we thank them.

Go to a place that feels holy and right. Begin freely speaking a prayer of gratitude to this unseen protector. Let the words spill spontaneously from your tongue. Keep going. Begin with thanks, and see where the river of words takes you. Stay with this for as long as you can, and then fall silent. Look for a sign from the Otherworld that shows you the rite is finished.

Rite III: The Crow Soothsayer

At the end of our story, the boy is resurrected in the form of a talking crow. In many cultures crows have long been associated with the dead. They haunt us. Their eyes are deep and timeless. Their shrill call cannot be ignored. With the aid of his mother's spirit, the boy is reborn in a wilder form, a shape his wicked stepmother cannot harm. Like the bone that sings the story of the princess's death, this crow speaks a truth that cannot be unheard.

For our final rite, go to a place where you might hear the birds sing. If you can go during those liminal hours that flank sunrise or sunset, go then. Be safe. Carry with you only a question about your life right now, perhaps even a question about your place in the world story. Reflect on the ancestral work we have done thus far in the Night House, and name a question that feels important.

When you can hear the birds, listen. Let your inner narrator go quiet, and just listen to the winged ones. What do you hear? If their bird sounds were voices, what would they be saying? How are they answering your question? Allow the birds to gift you a strange truth. Take your time; it might not come quickly or easily. When you hear it, you'll know. Offer gratitude, last, to the birds for speaking, and carry this new knowing into the world.

The Wisdom of the Dreaming Time

The veil is thin, so they say, at mid-autumn. This is the boundary between the living and the dead, yes, but it is also the wall between who we know ourselves to be and who we are becoming. In our dreams, this veil is always thin. Our dreams show us the next steps, the soon-to-come possibilities, the about-to-open doors, and the next opportunities available to us.

Reflect on your work with these Rites of the Blackbird, with the story of the shapeshifting boy who met his end but was reborn. Notice the ancestral stories that stepped forward and wanted to be seen and heard. Notice the memories that fed you for a time. You might ask yourself now if you can recall any dreams where it seemed a spirit came through, where it seemed more like a transmission, a conversation, than a dream. When you feel ready, cross a threshold, taking care, and once you have stepped across that creek bed or walked over the bridge, freely speak a prayer that begins like this: *I have met the blackbird spirit, and now I know...*

Our time in the bone cellar has ended, for now. We prepare to ascend from the depths, from the places of deep shadow where the bloody wells lay hidden away until the warrior bird-women find them and spill their secrets by firelight. Now we find the spiral staircase that leads up, up, up to the tower of spirit, to the place where wise nightmares are brewed, the devil is teacher, and long braids are severed. Bring with you all you have gathered in the Night House so far, toss some wood on the fire in the hearth, and head upward to the forbidden places where dreams always come true.

LESSONS FROM THE BONE CELLAR

Our stories will outlive us.

Our creative innocence must be protected.

Death is not the end.

The old stories contain powerful charms.

The stories of your ancestors are alive in you.

Part III

The Spirit
Tower

Chapter 10

———✦———

The Thirteenth Wise Woman

*And one day, just a moment ago, an old woman came from
her place at the edge of the village, her ears replete with listening, a
mouth of fresh-cut meadow flowers, and told us to light the kindling.
Once it was dark and the little ones were drifting under their antelope
robes, the strange one loped forward into the light of the flames
and stood in front of the village. She said: Once upon a time.
Once upon a time. Once upon a time. So she said.
And she told us the story of ourselves back to ourselves.*

MARTIN SHAW, *Scatterlings*

Here our Night House journey begins its third and final stage. We
take to the tower, and we consider what it means to be wise. In
the old stories, including fairy tales and myths, we often encounter a
bitter hag-woman who is both feared and revered. Those who shun her
suffer dire consequences, but those who are kind may be rewarded. At
times she is very like a trickster character, amoral in her actions, blessing some and cursing others, with no discrimination. We can look at
her, this wandering hag, as a force of nature, and understand that to be
truly wise means — no matter how *good* we consider ourselves to be —
to take great care when walking alone in her wilderness.

In the old Irish and Scottish stories, we meet the Cailleach, the
witch of winter who dwells in the rough places. She is inextricably

bound to place, to the elements, and to the ground. She is the elder feminine made manifest in land, sea, and sky, the mystical and supernatural forces of weather and wonder. Her lore is the lore of place, and her wisdom is older than ancient, a knowing before knowing. Part of the Cailleach's mythology is her ability to save travelers on the road or leave them for dead and, like a sudden storm, she might let good people die young while the ne'er-do-wells live long. She makes us question what is truly fair. She makes us wonder whether the human animal simply created the idea of fairness, conjuring notions of justice from thin air to sustain the overculture's power. In fairy tales this fearsome hag-woman must be treated well, but even then there is no insurance against her power, no protection from her wrath.

In our first story from the Spirit Tower, we meet the Thirteenth Wise Woman, the witch who was shunned. This familiar fairy tale unfolds around her as she creates the conditions for the maiden's initiation when she was just an infant. She weaves the fate of the little girl before the child can even walk or speak. Like the feared Moirai or Three Fates, those weird sisters who weave the world alive, the Thirteenth Wise Woman in our guiding story commands a fierce respect; when she does not receive what she is due, when she is eschewed by the king, she acts accordingly. She cares little for the innocence of the daughter, and she keeps her terrible promise.

To tend this story means to consider the nature of fate, the threads of your life that were spun long before you were born, the contracts of soul and family that both liberate and limit. Here we wonder about why we were born here and now, and how we can excel within the confines of our so-called lot. We might wonder whether the apparent limitations we were given, what we might call our fate, are really the boundaries our soul set for us in order to best fulfill our destiny, our greatest glory. The wise women in these old stories who have the power to reward and destroy, who spin the fate of the innocents and care little for what is fair and just, do so only to see destiny fulfilled. We see our own fate in the face of the wise woman. In her song we hear prophecies of the yet-to-come for us, for our people, and for our world.

Invitations for Tale-Tending: Inside Fate's House

This first room in the Spirit Tower is covered in roses, thorns, and the red thread of fate. Before you meet this story of roses and the long sleep, reflect on the nature of this thing called fate. Recall the archetype of the trickster, the character who is least predictable in the old stories, and how the old wise hag sometimes walks the way the trickster walks. The word *fate* has an etymological tie to the word *fae*, or that Irish trickster some call *faery* and, again, a fairy tale is really a fate story. The trickster bends the story, twists the fate of the characters, and creates the conditions for destiny to be realized.

If fate limits and destiny liberates, then destiny operates within the confines of fate. Fate gives just the right shape, just the right length of thread, to weave what must be woven. Fate speaks to predestination, and we find no comfort in choicelessness, but destiny speaks to our freedom. The foundation and the walls have been carefully constructed for us, but the spirit called Destiny dwells freely here. Before you meet the thirteenth hag, consider this, the next lesson from the Night House: What we do inside fate's house is up to us.

What we do inside fate's house is up to us.

Envision now this image: an empty spinning wheel, threadless and still. Where and how do you see this spinning wheel? How do you feel when you see or otherwise sense this image? If it could speak, what would it tell you here and now? Write this lesson down, the spinning wheel's message to you.

STORY ALTAR: THE TIES THAT BIND

Create an altar for this story, if you feel so called. Include roses and thread, wildflowers and thorns. Place symbols that, to you, represent the "ties that bind." Fate, they say, is family, after all. Include symbols on your story altar of moments in your life that felt like the stuff of fate, like there was no choice but to go a certain way. You might also include symbols of woven things to signify the grander tapestry of which we are all a part. What if, like little Brier Rose's fate in this story, there are some chapters in our lives that were always going to unfold? Stay curious about the truth of this statement as our story begins: The bargain was already made before we took our first breath.

Brier Rose

Once alive and then dead and now alive again, there was a queen who longed for a daughter with her whole heart. Each night, she dreamt of a babe crowned in roses and full of life. Each morning, she woke and prayed into the dawn that her greatest wish be granted but, with every new moon, the queen's blood came.

Every spring equinox, the queen's sorrow would be particularly great, for she would sense the seeds quicken belowground and see the pale-green sprouts unfurl and reach for the sun; she lamented the fallowness of her womb's red soil and envied the earth's effortless fertility. One year, one equinox morning, she again watched the house her body so carefully built for her unnamed babe collapse and pour from between her thighs in a jewel-red stream, and she was consumed by a grief so great she thought she should best leave behind her old life.

She took to the woods, as wild women often do. She told no one, and she headed into the haunted borderlands where she knew the ghosts roamed free.

They won't look for me here, she thought, walking the otherworldly road. For hours she wept and she walked, witnessed by the forest spirits who understood her sorrow, who had seen such things before. As dusk swept its shadows through the woodland, the queen firmly decided she would not return. She called the roots of a weathered oak her new castle, the moss her throne, and she curled up to sleep at the crossroads between who she had been and who she was becoming.

She woke without waking then, hearing the sound of swiftly rushing water. The light was dim and holy, as it was in the hour before sunrise, and she moved toward the water's song. So loud was the water, the queen expected to find an immense river, but all she found there in her dreamscape was a fairy pool, no deeper than a puddle of rain; as soon as she saw it, the sound fell silent. The wind died, and the birds ceased their morning calls.

All around her a strange mist swirled in spectral waves, and the queen stepped to the edge of the water, gazing down at her own reflection and seeing herself still asleep beneath the oak.

I'm dreaming, she thought, and just then a fat frog leapt from the fairy pool and landed at the queen's feet. She gasped and nearly fell over, suddenly remembering all the stories of these haunted woodlands. The dead walk heavy here, they say. The tricksters rule the liminal hours, and nothing is as it seems.

"Hello, my queen," the frog said in a gruff voice, lighting a pipe and taking a seat on a stump. He was a gray-bearded little fellow with bags under his eyes. "Why have you been crying?"

"I…I," the queen started, remembering the dangers of speaking to talking animals but unable to resist spilling all her secrets to this strange creature. This was only a dream, after all. "I long for a daughter with all that I am, but she's never come. I grow old now, and my wish slips between my fingers like sand."

The frog puffed on his pipe, and the light in the forest shone with a warm, golden glow. The queen began to weep, and her tears fell into the fairy pool once, twice, and thrice. As soon as the third tear fell, the frog leapt back into the water, saying, "Wake up, queen. Your wish is granted."

The next thing the queen saw was a brown rabbit hopping along the road and the rays from the rising sun beaming between the trees. She was still lying on her mossy throne, the roots of the oak pressing into her ribs. She pulled herself upright and listened; there was no sound of water. She walked to where the fairy pool had been, but the ground was dry.

Only a dream, she thought again, but a small seed of hope had been planted in her heart. She pressed her hand into her low belly and wondered if there was a new life inside. As soon as she had that thought, a lone green shoot rose up from the ground where the water had been, budding and sprouting a single red rose in the space between the queen's inhale and exhale. She smiled, whispered a prayer of gratitude to her ancestors, and began the journey home to the castle, to the king, and to her old life.

The next new moon, her blood didn't come, and the frog's words came true. Spring turned to summer, and the queen dreamt of roses night after night. When the witching moons of autumn came, the queen knew she would call her daughter Brier Rose, and she dreamt of a glamorous blessing ceremony to celebrate her newborn.

"We will invite the thirteen wise women," the queen said to the king. "We'll serve them on plates made of gold, and each of them will bestow a gift upon our beautiful Brier Rose. Make it so. Send the invitations."

On the longest night, the queen went into labor. The bells were rung, and the kingdom prayed for the mother and child. All over the land, though it was deep winter, roses began to bud and bloom. After many hours, the flame-haired Brier Rose was born, healthy and well, and the king readied the invitations for the thirteen wise women.

The next day, the king was handing the invitations to his messenger just as one of the servants hobbled toward him breathless with panic, carrying a heavy load of golden plates.

"King! I have terrible news! There are only twelve plates! We've no time to order more. What will we do?"

The king thought about serving one of the wise women on a clay plate while the rest ate off their golden plates, knew it would be a great insult, and made the poor choice to send only twelve invitations.

"Problem solved," the king said, tossing one of the invitations over his shoulder. "Don't tell the queen."

In early February the day of the blessing feast arrived. Candles were lit in the snow all around the castle, and roses covered every surface. One by one, the wise women began arriving, some on horseback, one inside a garish carriage shaped like a pumpkin, others flanked by cats, riding on wolves, and flying on brooms. The queen counted them, these wild ones who spoke the old language, who remembered a time before time.

"There are only twelve," she said to the king, and he waved a dismissive hand.

"One of them couldn't make it," he lied.

The feast went smoothly, with the twelve wise women full and fed by midnight. The scent of roses was so thick in the air, all the guests swooned as if they were drunk, and the queen thought it was time to present her greatest blessing, the beauty that was her babe, her long-held wish come true.

"May I present my daughter," she said. "The Brier Rose."

The wise women gasped at the child's fiery hair. She was dressed in a long gown, much too long for her small body, stitched from the softest pink and red rose petals. The queen passed her beloved bundle to the first wise woman, and she bestowed her gift.

"Oh, sweet Brier Rose. May you always know love in this life," she said, tracing a symbol on the baby's cheek and passing her to the next wise woman.

"May you be well protected, even as you sleep," the second wise woman said, handing her to the third, who said, "May you stay true to who you are and marry a man of your choosing."

The blessings continued, with each wise woman enchanting the princess with great gifts and worthy protections while the queen watched and wept, so full of joy that her prayers were finally answered.

Finally, Brier Rose was blessed by the eleventh wise woman, who was handing her to the twelfth, just as a shrill howl shook the room.

"How dare you?" It was the shunned wise woman who had never received an invitation. The queen was confused as the king began making his apologies, but the shunned wise woman would not hear him. She took her black hood down and stepped boldly toward the table, snatching little Brier Rose from the hands of the eleventh wise woman.

"I curse you, child," she hissed. "On this day, I curse you. On your nineteenth birthday, you shall prick your finger on a spinning wheel and take your last breath, never to wake again. Such is your fate."

The queen fainted, unable to face such terror, and the king prostrated himself at the shunned wise woman's feet, begging her to undo the horrible hex. She said nothing more, stepping over the king, raising her hood, and leaving the room stunned in silence.

A long hour passed, and the queen began to stir awake.

"Give me the child," the twelfth wise woman, the only one who had yet to bestow a blessing, whispered. "I'm afraid I can't undo the curse, but I can soften it." She pressed her finger into the babe's heart. "On your nineteenth birthday, you will prick your finger on a spinning wheel, and you will sleep for a hundred years."

The wise women nodded with approval, for this was all that could be done.

The king spent the next year ridding the kingdom of every spinning wheel. He had massive fires in all four corners of the land, where spinning wheels were burned to ash, and owning one was punishable by death. Strangely, the king kept just one spinning wheel, locking it in the cellar in the room behind the red door and forbidding anyone to go inside.

As Brier Rose grew older, she was told never to go down to the cellar, but as the years passed no one could quite remember why. The memory of the terrible blessing feast was fading, and the curse was too terrible to be true. Slowly but surely, the king and queen forgot the wise woman's hex, and by the time Brier Rose was twelve years old, no one in the castle remembered the fate that was to befall her in seven years.

On that very day, on Brier Rose's twelfth birthday, the king and the queen left to go gather roses for their daughter's celebration, as they always did, the peculiar winter roses that bloomed only around the castle and only on the longest night. Left alone, the princess felt her first blood come, and she felt called to go into the haunted woodland.

Never before had she gone to the woods alone, but she felt very changed today. The forest seemed to whisper her name, and she took to the otherworldly road, as her mother had done so many years before.

They won't look for me here, she thought, and she walked for hours while the sun sank low in the sky. At the crossroads where the queen had fallen asleep, Brier Rose grew quite tired and lay down upon the moss.

She woke to the sound of water, moving toward it, only to find a small fairy pool. She looked into the water, expecting to see her reflection but seeing herself curled asleep beneath the oak. As before, the bearded frog leapt from the water, and the princess fell back, startled.

This time, the frog spit a small key onto the ground, a silver key tied to a red ribbon.

"Keep it secret," the frog said. "Tell no one," he warned, disappearing under the water.

The next thing the princess saw was the little brown rabbit hopping along the road, the full moonlight shining on its back. She was beneath the oak, and the silver key was in her hand. Tying the ribbon around her neck, she tucked the key inside her dress.

For years she wore the key, never daring to use it, but on the eve of her nineteenth birthday, she dreamt of the room with the red door. The next morning, she woke to find the castle nearly empty, as everyone had left to prepare for her birthday celebration. Her parents were out gathering roses, and her thoughts were consumed by her dream.

It was late morning, nearing eleven, and the princess crept down the stairs to the cellar. Removing the key from her neck, where it'd been hidden for seven years, she unlocked the forbidden door. Inside, the Thirteenth Wise Woman spun away at a spinning wheel.

"What is that?" The princess had never seen a spinning wheel before.

"It's where your fate gets woven," the woman answered. "Go ahead. Touch it."

The princess pressed her finger lightly to the spindle, and it drew blood. She gasped and immediately fell to the floor asleep.

Everyone who was still within the castle walls closed their eyes, all falling into the deepest sleep of their lives. Cookpots still bubbled, the fires still cracked in their hearths, but every living and breathing creature slept. Cats, dogs, the horses in their stables, even the flies on the wall fell asleep.

For those arriving at the castle, as soon as they crossed the threshold, sleep overtook them. Soon there was a heap of sleeping bodies piled high in front of the castle gate, and the king and queen returned to join their sleeping court. As the guests arrived for Brier Rose's celebration, they too fell into a deep sleep, the roses they had gathered falling to the ground all around them.

In the weeks that passed, people came to the castle to discover why their people had not returned, but they too would fall asleep. In less than one moon's time, a rumor spread that the castle was cursed and that no one should travel there. In the following years, every so often a brave and arrogant person would decide they would be the one to solve the mystery, but they too would never return.

Thorny rosebushes began to crawl around the castle walls, weaving in and out of the windows and cracking through the foundation. In ten years' time, the castle was completely covered in rosebushes. In twenty years' time, few remembered the castle ever existed. Another king took the old king's place, people who remembered the cursed castle grew older, and the stories of the place grew more fantastical and twisted. Thirty, forty, and fifty years went by, leaving only a few old ones who remembered the castle even existed.

Ninety years to the day that the great sleep began, an old man appeared in the forest, a bearded fellow smoking a pipe. He would greet travelers as they passed and tell them about the castle. He said he was very old but, when he was a child, a castle stood there that housed a beautiful princess and great wealth. He would tell anyone who listened of the bounty that was there, pointing in the castle's direction and leaving them with a warning.

"But don't dare go," he'd say. "If you do, it will be the death of you."

Everyone he told was so curious, though, so full of greed and boldness, they just couldn't help it. They would go to the castle, finding only a field of towering brambles, and begin to cut their way through the thorns. As soon as they were deep enough inside, the thorns would move and writhe and tighten, squeezing in on them and piercing their skin until they died.

This went on for ten years, and more and more bodies rotted in the brambles around the castle. One day, on the one-hundredth anniversary of the great sleep's beginning, a wild man happened upon the old one in the woods. As he did with all the others, the old man told the wild one about the castle, but this time he ended his story in this way: "But don't dare go until you know it's safe."

The wild man thanked the old one for his direction and went to the castle. He stood at the field of brambles for hours, sensing something was coming. It was late morning, nearing eleven, and all this happened at once: Brier Rose, having slept for exactly one hundred years to the hour, opened her eyes. The thorny brambles surrounding the castle all bloomed into soft red roses, and the wild man could easily pass through them. Every living creature inside the castle walls opened their eyes, disoriented and confused.

The wild man made his way through the sea of waking bodies and bleary-eyed creatures, heading straight to the room with the red door as if someone was calling him. He found her there, Brier Rose, and she remembered she had dreamt of him often during her long sleep.

"Is it you?" she asked.

"It's me," he said.

And they lived happily ever after, made so, as we all are, by gratitude and grief.

The Three Rites of the Rose Child

The plot of this tale is familiar. The faulty bargain is made by the parents before the babe is even born, but it is that very deal that shapes the child's fate. Brier Rose's father insults the witch, but even before the gold plate goes missing, it is the mother who encounters the fairy spirit, the fae, the fate. While the maiden chooses to use the key and to enter the forbidden room, where she pricks her finger, we know it was not really a choice at all. Even the maiden's name foretells how her story will unfold. The symbol of the prolific roses is powerful, and we see the ways in which the roses shield the maiden in her incubatory sleep, in her metamorphosis. Fate found her. The bargain was fulfilled, and now, upon waking, the rest is up to her.

After meeting this story, a story you may have met before, what do you still wonder? If you reflect on this tale as if hearing it for the first time, what question bubbles to the surface of your psyche? The ever-after has come. What question persists? Write this question down.

Consider why this might be the vital question of your life now. Why does this question feel important to you? What does this tale illuminate for you, and what's underneath it? Reword this question about the story slightly now to be more personal to you, more specific to your life.

Look then to your message from the spinning wheel, the lesson you wrote down before the once-upon-a-time came. How is this message a peculiar answer to your question? Let this be your starting point, your first step as you begin the Rites of the Rose Child.

Rite I: Setting a Place for the Hag

The symbolic action of leaving gifts for tricksters and spirits so their more destructive powers pass you by exists across traditions and cultures. In voudou, gifts are left at the crossroads for the death bringers. In Irish culture, milk and bread are left on the windowsill for the fae. A farmer leaves the "pooka's lot" in the field so the crops are not poisoned, and the list of dangerous trickster spirits and the gifts they require goes on.

In our story, the king and queen set no place for the Thirteenth Wise Woman. She receives no invitation, and this is their downfall. Here we learn that we must set a place for the hag. We must leave a gift in the field and an offering at the crossroads. However, this is not done in search of blessing or reward; it is done to appease and to remember. When we set a place for the hag, we set the conditions to accommodate her, if needed. She might not come. The fairies might not drink the milk, but should they decide to come to the house, their gift will be there.

Setting a place for the wild hag does not make her more or less likely to arrive; it is an act of remembrance. We understand that life contains many uncertainties, many shadows that haunt our path unseen and unnoticed, and it behooves us to remember that the trickster is always afoot. This knowing helps us stay flexible, unwed to our best-laid plans and prepared for all manner of weather.

For this first Rite of the Rose Child, set a place for the hag. You might do this at your altar or your dining table. Set a place for her, the Thirteenth Wise Woman. Show her that if she happens to stop by, she has a place at your table. Like our shadows, when we refuse to see them, their destructive power increases. With this first rite, look the hag right in the eye. Make room for her. Pour her a glass of wine or honeyed tea, and straighten her fork and spoon.

After you set her place, leave it there for three days. On the third day, carry the drink you poured for her to your garden or another wild place. Pour the liquid in a circle on the ground and speak a prayer to your ancestors to protect you and your kin as your thread of fate stretches long through deep time.

Rite II: The Compact of the Motherline

There is an often unwitnessed intelligence in the names you were given, the names you chose for yourself, and the names of your people. If you look at your legal name, what meanings can you derive from it? Be objective, and write down the meanings behind your first, middle, and last names. If there are other names you go by now, chosen names or married names, dig into the meaning of those words too. What do you notice?

This is only the beginning of this, our second Rite of the Rose Child. In our story Brier Rose is named as such because of the color of her hair, but her mother was dreaming of roses before she was born. During her incubatory and initiatory sleep, she is protected by the roses. The roses grow and rise to keep her safe. They provide a boundary. Like fate's house, like the containers we are given, we are not only limited by them but at times protected by them.

If you know your mother's name, look to the word story she was born to. What meaning can you derive from her full name, maiden and married, if applicable. If you know your mother's mother's name, your maternal grandmother, do the same here. What ancestral story do you see if you look at the names inherent in the motherline? What can you ascertain about your role, your fate, even your soul's contract, if you look at your name's meaning within the context of the larger motherline story?

If it feels right, you might write the following on a sheet of paper, and leave it near the place you set for the hag: I am (the meaning of your current name), once (the meaning of any old names), daughter of (the meaning of your mother's name), granddaughter of (the meaning of your maternal grandmother's name), and great-granddaughter of (the meaning of your maternal grandmother's mother's name). Leave the paper there for a time, holding the tension of whatever realizations come. Look to your dreams, noticing if any symbols emerge from the name story while you sleep.

Rite III: The Dreamer's Message

We dream in small stories. Think of how deeply Brier Rose dreamt for those one hundred years, the stories she was a part of during her unconscious initiation. Think of the wisdom she received during her long dreaming time.

We know that our dreams are often prophetic. What if these dreams were sent to us, or rather *back* to us, from our own wise and future selves in order to orient us toward our best self, a purpose we are meant to fulfill, or indeed, our fate? This wonder breaks the bonds of linear time, of course, but if we hold the tension of *what if*, if we consider that this could be true, we unlock a wealth of wisdom, the very wisdom we possess at some point in the yet-to-be.

For this last rite, our strangest ritual yet, all you need to do is look for a telling dream tonight. Whenever you are reading this, make note of the date and, upon waking tomorrow, reflect on any dreams you remember. Write them down, and we will revisit them later. Know that you do dream, whether or not you remember these dream-stories. When your write your dreams down, even when you write, "I do not remember what I dreamt," it is very like setting a place for the hag; you are giving the dream room. People who frequently say that they don't dream tend not to remember their dreams in part because they leave no room for them in their conscious world. Leave room for the dream. Tomorrow morning, set the intention to spend just a minute or two writing down what you remember, even if you remember very little.

To Bend Time

We will continue our dreamwork here in the Spirit Tower, noticing the plot of our dreams, the crises we encounter, and the helpers who join us in the dreaming time. We will consider the validity of linear time and the wisdom in allowing it to bend, to loop, to even break apart. As our visit to the Night House draws to a close, we look to the way these stories are shaping our experience, influencing our memory of our personal plotlines, and allowing us to re-member, to reorganize, the past.

If you reflect now on the strange Rites of the Rose Child, what do you notice? These rites are a bit unsettled, a bit unfinished. If there is tension in your body when you reflect on these rituals, imagine a rose growing there in that place right now. Breathe deep. When you feel ready, cross a threshold, stepping through a doorway or between two oaks. As you do, upon the crossing, speak a prayer that begins as follows: *I have met the thirteenth wise woman, and now I know...*

Our next story is a tale of a journey initiated by a dream, a dream we might call fated. Like fairy tales, dreams have been robbed of their perceived value, but it was not always this way. Dreams, in many indigenous cultures, were very valid motives for making decisions, even for entirely changing the direction of one's life. Like the shadow, like the Thirteenth Wise Woman, like fate's contract that is somehow hidden inside our name, we cannot dismiss our dreams; they're alive in us, whether or not we acknowledge them.

Chapter 11

The Ruined One's Dream

*We are on the cusp of a revolution
in our thinking about time and mind.*

ERIC WARGO, *Precognitive Dreaming*

Those who try to firmly hold the old stories, carving them into definable pieces and surgically separating them from their whole, often fail in their attempts. While there are literary fairy tales whose written origin is understood, even those stories often share discernible threads with the tales in the oral tradition, the stories whose birthplace and first mother are shrouded in mystery. Fairy tales, these small fate stories, were woven slowly, spun by the tongues of generations, shaped and reshaped by each teller and their unique intent, by each listener who told and retold the tale, adding this and omitting that, diluting one message and amplifying another.

The oldest fairy tale is likely thousands of years old. While we cannot know and name the precise origin of many of these stories, the exact moment the fires were lit and the story was told for the first time, we can say with certainty that these stories came forth in a time that preceded our modern conveniences. These old stories emerged in the dark. That they were able to survive and thrive, that we still speak of them today is nothing short of remarkable.

The worlds of the tellers from long ago differed considerably from ours; theirs was a time when nature's omens were accepted as truth and the intelligence of a dream was taken seriously. In her book *Shadow and Evil in Fairy Tales*, Marie-Louise von Franz considers that fairy tales originated as someone's dream, a dream that was recounted and consequently remolded, formed not only by the fears and wants of the teller but also by the landscapes in which they lived. Those who discount the power of story would do well to remember that we dream in story.

While we sleep, we are immersed in a magickal narrative. Our dreams begin with a once-upon-a-time, with an exposition and a clear setting, only to progress toward a certain crisis or climax. We meet a problem we are meant to resolve, a task we are meant to complete, like a child in the house of Baba Yaga. We are given a challenge and, sometimes, we meet that challenge well. Some dreams come to a timely resolution, an ever-after we sense is somehow medicinal. Our dreams are always trying to heal, protect, or, if nothing else, change us, and this is true whether or not we recall the whole story that meets us in the dreaming time.

These little night stories act on us and through us during our waking hours, and how could they not? In his book *Precognitive Dreamwork and the Long Self*, Eric Wargo asserts that humans and animals essentially premetabolize the future every night in their dreams, behaving in a way that will inevitably fulfill the dream's prophecy. This theory counters our glorious notions of free will, of course, but it also wonderfully shatters conceptions of linear time. When we question the inevitability of linear time, that the effect will inevitably follow the cause, a certain tension arises in our minds but, if we pay attention, our body experiences a liberation.

In our next story from the Spirit Tower, we find fate fulfilled because of a telling dream. We hold the strange wonder that, just maybe, parts of our lived stories are predetermined, are the stuff of fate, and it is through the magickal mechanism of the dreaming time that we follow fate's thread. To tend this story means to suspend our disbelief, to make a little space in our minds where time does not move in the way we might predict, where the yet-to-come already influences the present moment.

Invitations for Tale-Tending: Time's Trick

The next room in the Spirit Tower is built from shredded calendars and broken clocks. Most of us already have ample proof that linear time is at least malleable, stocked inside the house of our memory. The problem is, we are socialized to dismiss these moments almost as soon as we live them. Hours pass, and we question whether we really foresaw that bizarre occurrence that just happened. As children we might share with our caregivers a telling dream that comes to pass, but the unfavorable reaction by these authority figures is sufficient to keep us quiet the next time a prophetic dream or waking vision arises. We rush to dismiss what we know is true. We do not want to seem too weird, but now we know that *weird* comes from *wyrd*, which means "fated."

Arguments against the prophetic nature of dreams often cite that these little night stories do not precisely predict the yet-to-be; pieces of them seem prophetic, but the dream's aspects that end up not fitting in to the lived experience are enough to dismiss the apparent precognition. Wargo asserts that this is because dreams build "future towers out of past bricks." The dream must use the preexisting materials, shaped from our memories, to which it has access. Anything that the dream cannot build from the existing material will not translate precisely, hence the dream seems to contain some prophecy and other odd tidbits that do not end up coming to fruition.

If we accept that dreams predict *some* aspects of the future but cannot accurately show us the *all*, the whole of the exact story we are about to live, we can accept that fate does sit alongside destiny, that some stories are already scripted, but others are as yet unwritten. Our next lesson from the Night House shows us this truth, that dreams illuminate the yet-to-come. Dreams show us the part of our as-yet-unlived story we are both meant to foresee and inevitably will experience. This means that not all fated parts of our lives are shown to us in dreams, but it also means that much is left to our own free will. Again, what we do inside fate's house is up to us.

Dreams illuminate the yet-to-come.

Envision this strange image now: a once-grand but now ruined estate, an immense and crumbling house. How do you see this place? What season is it? What time of day? How does this place sound and smell, and how do you feel there? If this image could speak, what would it tell you? Write this message down, the message from the ruined house.

Story Altar: Ode to the Dreamer

Build a small altar to this short story now. Include symbols you have met in your dreams, especially any that seem to recur. Also include symbols of moments when linear time seemed to fall apart for you, when you walked in the woods for what seemed to be only an hour but nearly a day had passed, or when a friend's premonition seemed to come true. Build this altar as a symbolic action of opening space for wonder around time, dreams, and the nature of our hours.

The Ruined One's Dream

Once in a time gone, gone, and now again here, there lived a man who was born into wealth. No one had taught him how to manage his money and, sadly, after his father died the man lost all he owned except his grand house. He toiled in the hot sun day after day, doing whatever he could in exchange for food, and his house fell into great disrepair. The roof began to cave in, the once-majestic fountain would no longer hold water, and his gardens withered and died. No matter how hard he worked, he never seemed to have any money.

One night he had a dream, and in this dream he was told he would regain his fortune in Cairo, so without any business or family to keep him in Baghdad, he left his house and journeyed to a place he had never been.

As soon as he arrived, he was badly beaten and thrown in prison. The guard, about to take the ruined man's life, asked him, as he lay bleeding, "Why are you here?"

To the guard's surprise, the man began laughing. "I dreamt I would find my fortune here, so I came. Some fortune I have found!"

The guard began laughing too and took pity on the ruined man, saying, "Oh, my dear man. I have dreamt night after night for many years of a grand house surrounded by fallowing gardens and a treasure of gold and silver buried beneath its broken fountain. I have dreamt of this but was never brave enough to seek it out."

The ruined man was shocked at the guard's words but said nothing, and the guard freed him and gave him enough money to get home to Baghdad.

As soon as he arrived, he dug beneath the fountain and found his family's vast fortune just where the guard had dreamt it was.

He lived happily ever after, made so, as we all are, by gratitude and grief.

The Three Rites of the Dreamer

This story's plot beautifully illuminates the nature of prophetic dreams. They orient us on a path that will fulfill a truth, but the dream itself is not a literal script of the yet-to-come. The dreamer in our story set out on a journey because of his dream, a journey that seemed to fail, to bring about even greater ruin. In the end, if he had not been inspired to travel because of his dream, he may never have found the wealth buried under his fountain.

We might wonder: Why would he not just dream of the treasure under his fountain and save himself the trip and the consequent ordeal of being imprisoned? To this we can only say that dreams work in bizarre ways, that there are experiences we are meant to live. Perhaps he would have wasted his newfound wealth had he not been affected by his experiences in Cairo. Perhaps some hidden pieces of the story explain why it had to be.

What else do you wonder about this tale? The ever-after has come. What question remains for you? Name this question. Write it down.

Now ask, Why is this my question? What lies underneath this question, and why is that my wonder? Reshape the question slightly to be about your life or the world, a question that is no longer obviously specific to the story. After you have this new question, look to your lesson from the ruined house, the message you wrote down before you met this story. How is this message an answer, though likely an odd one, to your question? Let this be your starting point, as we begin the Rites of the Dreamer.

Rite I: Sending the Dream

Recall your work with the Brier Rose story, with the Rites of the Rose Child. In particular, recall the third rite, the Dreamer's Message. Were you able to remember that telling dream? Depending on how much time has passed since you moved through that practice, you might want to return to your notes and see what you wrote down. Perhaps you had a clear symbol or even a whole story. Perhaps you merely remember a color or a shape, a flash of some image you cannot quite grasp.

If you look to your notes, can you see when you moved through this practice? What date was it? Do you remember where you were that night as you slept?

When you are ready to move through this practice, be in a space where you will not be disturbed. Turn all ringers off. Press your fingertips lightly into your palms to open the hand chakras. Breathe. Close your eyes, and begin to imagine the image of a bright-red rose. See it clearly. Amplify the image. Make it brighter. Hold the rose image, and now begin to imagine yourself asleep wherever you were the night you moved through the last Rite of the Rose Child. Let it be part memory and part vision. See yourself asleep there, and begin to imagine you are sending the rose image to your dreaming self.

Hold your hands so that your palms are facing away from you, as if you are sending this energetic image to you in the dreaming time. Meet your past self there. You, as the wise and future self, are now gifting this rose image to the once-was self. Stay with this for at least twenty minutes, if you are able.

When it feels finished, you might speak a blessing or prayer to your past self. You know what has happened in your life since that date of the last Rite of the Rose Child, after all. What does your past self need to hear or remember?

Return now to your notes about the dream you had. Was any rose imagery present? The color red? A garden? Does anything else feel connected somehow to where you find yourself today? If you are holding a blue pen, for instance, did you dream of a blue pen? Take notice, and do not feel disheartened if there is no apparent connection between this day and that past moment. Leave room for this, your cosmic nod, to still arrive.

Rite II: The Hands of the Yet-to-Be

For our second Rite of the Dreamer, begin a practice of dream recall. Commit to staying with this practice for at least nine days. This is an intentional practice of recounting your dreams upon waking. When you do this regularly, you find you possess a whole navigation system that for most people unfortunately remains hidden, though it need not. When you wake, spend three minutes recalling and writing down what you dreamt the night before.

Include the presleep and postsleep visions, the hypnagogic and hypnopompic visions, respectively. Distinguish these, however, from your deep dreaming. As noted earlier, if you do not remember your dream, it does not mean you dreamt nothing; in this case, write down *I don't remember what I dreamt.* You still want to show the dream that you are giving it space in your waking life, even if you don't consciously remember it.

This small act of creating space for the dream upon waking allows the dream to participate in your day, to affect your waking time. If you believe in the butterfly effect, then even those three minutes spent tending to the dream will inevitably shape the rest of the day, for you and even for others. You spend a little time writing your dream down, so then you leave your house a little later than you normally would, for instance, and a path is set before you that would not have been there otherwise.

If dreams are sent to us from the future, then this simple act of recalling them and writing them down allows the future to participate in the present. If dreams are showing us only the fated future, that which is already predetermined, then tending to them puts us more in tune with what will come. These are uncomfortable wonders, of course, but what if our dreams, these small night stories, are far more important than we were told? Like fairy tales, dismissed as inconsequential children's stories, dreams have been made to operate in the shadows for some time. They have not been taken seriously, yet they are embedded in the human experience.

At the end of the nine days, see what you notice from your dreaming time notes. Are the dreams becoming clearer? Does a symbol or a setting recur? Have any of these dreams come to pass in your waking hours? Continue this practice beyond these nine days, if you can. Keep going, and you open a whole world where fate becomes just a bit less confining, a bit less mysterious, but still incredibly profound.

Rite III: The Dreamer's Spell

For our final Rite of the Dreamer, we will invite a dream to participate in a spell. You will need to consider first your intention. Reflect on all the work you have done, not only with this story, not only in the Spirit Tower, but in the whole of the Night House. As our time draws to a close in this hidden place of shadow and shine, notice what you feel oriented toward. What do you want to call in for yourself? This will be the last spell we cast, so discern what you sense is an important desire, and then begin to shape it.

Allow this desire to become like a scene from a story. Let your want become a mythic image. What do you see? Just as importantly, how do you feel in this vision, in this story scene? The feeling is important; it ensures the vision finds you well and whole. Feel the feeling. See what you see.

After you have named this story scene that is your vision, recall your recent dreams. If you can't recall any recent dreams, go back as far as you need to. Find one dream scene, one dream symbol, that feels strangely important. You do not even need to know why. Do not choose a dream that feels like a nightmare, however; choose a dream that gives you a sense of the strange, that invites wonder into the body. You do not need the whole plotline from the dream, just like you don't need to know the whole story behind your vision. In witchcraft the *how* often gets in the way of the *what*. In the spell container, do not worry about how you arrived at the moment you are calling in. Simply stay tuned in to the what, to the desire you are seeking and is also seeking you.

Now consider a mythic image from one of our Night House stories. Recall the potent images we met before we encountered the stories: the wild skins and the dark moons, the singing bones and the blackbirds. Which image steps forward now and wants to be included in the spell? What image emerges as telling and important, like an oracle, right now in this moment?

Last, recall our previous time-weaving spell when we braided the past, present, and future. Remember the role of the memory, the way it shared a feeling similar to your vision. Name a memory now, a memory that contains the feeling you have when you think of this new moment you are calling in. Remember, the feeling of the memory will likely seem a diluted form of the feeling of the vision, and this is as it should be. We want our visions to feel amplified and full of power, but the memories tend to feel less charged.

When you are ready, take stock of these four points: (1) the vision you are calling in, (2) the dream scene, (3) the image from an old story, and (4) the memory. Know them, these four points. The fifth and final point in our time-weaving spell will be the present moment, the here and now.

When you are ready, go into a wild place. Invite the protectors, the ancestors, and the unseen helpers. Speak a small prayer to the four directions, and then begin shifting your weight from one foot to the other. Begin chanting the following: "This, that, all. This, that, all. This, that, all." Keep going.

As you chant, as you move, begin to weave with time. Tend first to the present moment, and then visit the other points as if a pendulum were swinging from future to past, getting wider and wider each time it swings. At first, move from the present moment to the vision, back to the present moment, and to the memory. Stay with this for a few minutes, though you will not have a clear sense of time's passing. Keep going.

When you feel a slight shift, let the pendulum swing wider to include the dream and the image from the story. Now you are psychically dancing from the present moment, to the vision, to the dream, to the vision, to the present moment, to the memory, to the image from the old story, to the memory, to the present moment, and again to the vision. Keep going. Do not worry if you get confused or mix up the order of the five points. Stay with the chant and the movement, and trust.

You will know when linear time begins to crumble because you will start to see or otherwise sense the image from the old story in your vision. The memory will begin to feel like the vision, and the dream will suddenly seem more solid and true. Keep going. Notice any symbols that seem to penetrate your vision, and look to these as potentially prophetic images. Take care with yourself, and begin to slow down the psychic dance when it feels right. Slow down the rocking in your body, and slow the chant.

When you are ready, let your body be still. Let the chant go silent. Notice what you see and how you feel. Ground yourself by tending to your senses. Offer gratitude to the four directions, to the elements and the ancestors. Breathe, and seal your spell by placing an object on your altar that reflects your vision, the moment in the yet-to-be that you called in.

Night School

Dreams are our night school, a place where we learn about our fate, practice skills we are being called to hone, and encounter shadows we simply cannot see when we are fully awake. Who we are in dreams is not who we are in life *yet*. Like a character in a fairy tale, we begin a certain way in our dreams, only to be changed. We leave the dream someone new, and we wake with a little part of them taking up residence in our hearts.

If you reflect now on the Rites of the Dreamer, notice what you can. What realizations emerged, and where was there resistance? Allow yourself to draw no conclusions. Decide nothing for sure, but hold the tension of the *maybe, just maybe*. When you are ready, find a threshold and cross it mindfully, a symbolic action of stepping away from one story and into the next. After you cross, begin a small prayer with these words: *I have met the dreamer, and now I know...*

The next chapter invites you to consider two stories, two tales about wisdom, learning, healing, and shadow. Here we leave the rules of the overculture behind, especially the ones about what our life's work should be. The old stories show us what it means to really go to school, to hone skills no one can teach us, though space can be held *for* us. Here we outsmart the devils and carve our own sunward path to liberation.

Chapter 12

The Devil's School

Where you have a mythic image, it has been validated by decades,
centuries, or millennia of experience along that path, and it provides a
model. It's not easy to build a life for yourself with no model whatsoever.

JOSEPH CAMPBELL, *Pathways to Bliss*

An archetype is like a small god, an energetic force of pure essence, an *original form* that contains the spirit of a particular meaning. Archetypes are alive, and they live and breathe in stories. Like a ghost taking possession of a doll in order to regain some vaguely human shape, archetypal energies take hold of characters in the old stories. The survival of fairy tales, these fate stories, over so many generations may be credited in part to the immortality of certain archetypes. The archetype of the ruler or sovereign cannot be killed off, no matter how many kings and queens die in the old stories, and neither can the devil be defeated forever, no matter how many times we guess his name, no matter how many bargains are broken.

Every time someone prays, sings, or builds an altar to a deity, they pour a little water into the energetic well of power that is that deity. Similarly, every time a story is told, the archetypes that live inside the tale gain a little strength. Telling stories about devils, demons, and tricksters keeps them breathing and, after so many generations, those wells of power run deep. Of course, we know that the devil originated as a force of nature, the dark to the light, and that *demon* stems from *daemon*, which means "genius," the hidden intelligence that propels us, that constantly orients us toward our purpose.

Lessons about the old magick, as much as the old magick itself, are alive in these stories, and many fairy tales containing devils, demons, and apparently malevolent spirits have much to teach us about our own power, our unique genius, our embedded and inborn blueprint that follows and guards us. The oldest fairy tale is thought to be "The Smith and the Devil," a six-thousand-year-old story about a blacksmith who makes a deal with the devil in order to gain supernatural abilities. Stories that amplify the theme of learning or school and also contain a devil character can show us the truth of that thing called wisdom, the inextricable bind between our healing, our wounds, and our purpose in this life.

Invitations for Tale-Tending: One Specific Thing

Inside this room, the walls are lined with glass bottles full of spirits, and just here your own wise and future self sits singing your soul's song. Can you see these spirit bottles? In the Night House we have already considered the kinship between our gifts and our deepest wounds; the gift slow-dances with the ache, always. When we ready our gifts to be witnessed by the world, the sacred wound begins to bleed. Time and time again, as we move through life, we are tasked with sensing the trouble of our great gift, hearing the voices of the inner wicked stepsisters that tell us to stay hidden in the ashes, and we shine nevertheless.

The archetype, the original form, of the wounded healer contains the truth of the gift and the ache. Our story begins with both our soul's gold and the soul's rot, and we carry both as our personal myth unfolds. There is no healing without the wound, and the wound has much to show us about our particular genius, our unique daemon. We become who we needed when we were younger, when the wound was raw and fresh, but the scar still aches even in our wisdom; knowing this as a power source rather than a sign of defeat is a hard-won understanding. As we ready ourselves to leave the Night House, we consider one of its sharper lessons now: Each of us is here to heal one specific thing.

Each of us is here to heal
one specific thing.

This chapter invites you to meet two stories, both tales of devils and learning, of arriving at a certain wisdom no one else could ever possess. Before meeting these stories, envision a faceless shadow now, a shadow you somehow know to be your own. How else do you see this shadow? How sharp are the lines, and what is the background? What season do you seem to be in, and what hour of the day is it? Now allow this shadow to speak. What does it tell you? Write this down, the message from the shadow.

Story Altar: Ode to the Underworld School

As you ready yourself to attend the Black School and release the Spirit in the Bottle, build a small altar to the sacred wound, to the ache that endures. There is no need to name this wound or to attach any memory or story to it. Simply build a place for it to live alongside these stories. You might include cracked eggshells or broken pieces of glass. Light a candle then, and speak a small prayer, allowing only what wants to be seen to come forth.

The Spirit in the Bottle

Once in a time that was known and unknown, a woodcutter labored from dawn to dusk. For years the man struggled to save enough money to send his only son, a wild boy who lived close to the land, to school. When his child came of age, the woodcutter had just enough money to finance his son's studies.

"Learn a good trade, my boy," the woodcutter said. "Don't waste your time with art or some healing nonsense. If nothing else, you shall have a better life than me."

For three years the wild son studied law, business, and other fields he thought his father would approve of, but despite his diligence and desire to make his father proud, he found he could not follow any traditional path. His studies floundered, and without any degree or prospects to speak of, the boy came home. He found his father had become quite feeble while he had been away, and he worried that he did not have much time left on this earth.

"Oh, father," the wild son said. "Let me do your work for you today. I'll go into the forest and cut wood as you do, but you rest today."

The father refused, angry that his son had returned without a good trade.

"You've become soft and lazy in your time away," the father said. "You wouldn't know what to do."

The father and son bickered for a while and then decided they would both go into the woods. The son borrowed an axe from the neighbor, promising to return it in good condition, and they set out into the haunted woodland they knew so well. For hours they worked, the father working quickly and the son working slowly. At midday the father bid them both rest and eat their lunch.

"I'm going to go hunt for bird nests, Father."

"Nonsense. Stay and eat," the father ordered.

The son protested. "You rest and eat. I'm not hungry."

"If you don't rest now, you'll be no good to me this afternoon," the father countered, but his wild son was already walking away.

After he had walked a good long while, he happened upon a massive oak tree. The young man was enchanted by the tree, knowing it must be many hundreds of years old.

"What mysteries have you in your branches?" the man whispered, and he circled the tree, looking for a low branch to climb. As he walked, he began to hear a strange chirping sound from below his feet. Pressing his ear to the roots, he heard a voice.

"Help! Let me out!" the voice said, and the wild son knew it was coming from beneath the enormous roots.

"Let me out!" the voice repeated. "I'm under the roots. Just here!"

The wild son began to dig with his hands, and the voice grew louder and louder until he saw it: a small blue bottle. Unearthing the tiny vessel, he squinted to see a shadow bouncing around inside the glass.

"Let me out!" the spirit ordered again, and the wild son, having no knowledge of such things, pulled the cork.

Immediately, a shadow spilled from the bottle and stretched tall and wide in all directions. The dark figure was larger than the oak tree now, hovering over the wild son and hissing. The young man was not afraid, however, as he had no reason to fear this creature.

"Do you know what your reward is for releasing me?" the shadow said, and the wild man shook his head. "It's a broken neck."

The wild man stood, holding the bottle, and the shadow reached its arms toward him.

"Wait," he said. "Before you break my neck, if that is indeed my reward, I must be sure it was you who was in this bottle. How can I know you are the same spirit I just freed?"

The spirit said nothing, and the wild son kept talking.

"This bottle is so small, and you are as big as this oak tree, after all. Am I to believe that you fit inside this glass? You take me for a fool."

"It was me you freed, and I can prove it," the spirit said, immediately crawling back inside the bottle. The wild son put the cork back in and held the glass up to his eye.

"What are you doing?" the spirit howled. "Let me out!"

The wild son tucked the bottle back under the oak root and turned away. The sun was sinking low in the sky, and his father would be worried.

"Wait!" the spirit called to him. "If you let me out, I vow to give you a reward so great, you will have enough of all things for the rest of your days."

The wild son stopped and turned.

"How do I know you won't deceive me again?" he asked the spirit.

"You don't, but if you walk away now, you will always wonder if you've shunned your greatest gift in this life," the spirit answered. The wild son thought for a moment, listening to the night birds sing their waking song.

"Very well," he said finally, and he uncorked the bottle. Again the small shadow grew, this time even bigger than before.

"Here is your reward," the shadow said, handing the wild son a small tattered rag. "It doesn't look like much, but if you rub a wound with one edge of this cloth, it will be healed instantly. If you rub iron or steel with the other edge, it will immediately transform into pure silver."

The wild son said nothing, picked up his axe, and sent the sharp iron straight into the bark of the great oak tree. Still wordlessly, he pressed the edge of the cloth to the tree's wound, and it was instantly whole and healed. The man bowed to the spirit, the spirit bowed to the man, and the bargain was complete.

It was nearly dark by the time the son returned to his father, and his father admonished him for spending so much time away.

"Don't worry, Father," the son said. "Watch this." As he rubbed his axe with the cloth, it turned to silver, and then he struck a thin-limbed pine. Because the axe was silver, it bent nearly in half, and the father gasped and mocked him.

"What have you done? Now I have to pay the neighbor for his damaged axe!"

The wild son told him not to worry, and the two headed home in the dark.

"Go and try to sell the bent axe," the father said the next morning. "Take whatever you can get for it, and we'll need to earn the rest."

The wild son went to the goldsmith, who examined the silver axe, weighing it and eyeing the quality of the silver.

"This is worth more than I can give you," he said finally. "I only have three hundred talers, but this fine axe is surely worth four hundred."

"Give me the three hundred talers," the wild son said. "You can owe me the rest."

He headed home then, finding his father anxious by the fire.

"What does the neighbor want for his axe?" the son asked.

"One taler," the father said. "How much did you get for it?"

The wild son showed his father his fortune, saying, "Take two talers to the neighbor for his axe. You keep the rest and spend the rest of your life as you like."

The father was stunned, and the wild son recounted his time with the Spirit in the Bottle.

"Some risks are worth it, Father," he said, and he became the most famous healer in the world with his enchanted cloth.

And the wild son lived happily ever after, made so, as we all are, by gratitude and grief.

The Questions That Remain

In this story the son's wound is quite visible. He wants to make his father proud and, in his mind and the mind of his father, he fails. Only by moving through his quite personal ordeal is he able to uncover his great gift as a healer. Yet his time in school was not wasted, for he was able to wield some of the cunning tools he learned in order to trick the spirit. He leaves neither school nor the woods having fulfilled his purpose in life, but the great power of his gift is now visible.

Before we meet our second story, name the questions that remain. What do you still wonder about the story, about the son or his father, the spirit or even the neighbor whose borrowed axe allowed the rest of the tale to unfold? Name your wonder. Write it down, and ready yourself to go underground.

The Black School

Once and still, a dark dwelling was carved deep into the most ancient stone, a hidden place where innocents traveled to learn the forbidden ways. The underground staircase to the Black School was always changing, and many were forever lost on the journey. For those who did find this place of mysteries, the risk did not end with their arrival.

Inside the Black School there was no daylight, no sun to illuminate the truth of things, and the students saw only by way of fire. There were no teachers, no mentors, and no wilderness guides. All who came to the Black School did so to learn from old books, scripted with flaming letters and a disembodied, gray-haired hand that directed each lesson only by gesture, brought the meals, and managed the rhythms of the day and night.

Those who came to this place stayed for seven years, unable to leave early, and upon leaving, were the most powerful mages, healers, and witches known to the world. Rumored to belong to the devil himself, the Black School was both feared and revered, shunned and coveted. No deep knowledge comes without risk, after all, and each student knew well the risk they took going there.

Every seventh November on that thin day when the dead walk heavy, the students who had lived underground for so long, who had become the wisest among us, would begin their journey sunward, making their way up the winding staircase, shielding their eyes as they approached the great iron gate that was open only on that day, so that the graduating students could leave. All were permitted to pass through the gate except the very last student.

The rule of the Black School was that the last student to leave each seventh November belonged to the devil. The iron gate would slam shut before they could cross the threshold, and no one knew what would become of them after that; no one ever looked back to bear witness, and so it had gone for thousands upon thousands of years.

No one knows why it happened, but it happened that one year, a new arrival at the Black School, called Saemunder the Wise, decided he would outsmart the devil, and he spent the next seven years learning all he could about the ways of shadow, death, and darkness. When the time came for his class to leave the school, he told them he would be the last to go.

He loosened his cloak as the last of the students in front of him made their way through the iron gate, and then it all happened at once: As he felt hands grab at his cloak, he slipped from them and hurled himself over the threshold of the iron gate before it slammed closed. He was breathless on the ground but free.

"No! You are mine!" a voice hissed from the darkness.

Saemunder stood and walked back toward the gate, letting the sun cast a sharp shadow of his figure on the cave wall.

"Look!" he said, pointing at the shadow. "I am not the last to leave. There is your prize," and the devil snatched his shadow, keeping it there at the Black School forever.

The Three Rites of the Shadow School

In the story of the Black School, a sacrifice is made in exchange for the deep and otherworldly knowledge. Like in "The Smith and the Devil," that six-millennia-old fairy tale, the students of the Black School are knowingly dealing with the devil in order to gain supernatural powers. Learning such things comes with great risk, after all, but Saemunder dares to defeat the devil, to skip the sacrifice.

Now that the tale is over, what do you still wonder? Name the question that remains, the missing piece of the plot that feels significant to you. Write this question down.

Look at this question from the Black School and your former question from the Spirit in the Bottle. Is there any connection between them? Did you repeat a word, or do the two questions share a feeling? Take the questions now, and reshape them to be questions about your life, queries that are more personal to you now.

Recall your message from the shadow image, the words you wrote down before meeting these two tales. If you look at these two questions, how is your shadow message an answer to both of them? Draw no conclusions yet. Just wonder. What is revealed by these two question-and-answer pairings? Let this be your starting point, your orientation, as you begin the Rites of the Shadow School.

Rite I: Humor, Humble, Human

Our first rite is a ritual of reflection. The word *reflection* means "to bend back." We see our reflection in a mirror, we reflect on the past, but we also understand that the memories stepping forward when we recall previous chapters from our story more accurately reflect who we are now than they are precise, play-by-play recollections of our experience. We are constantly re-membering, reorganizing the past. We are constantly forming narratives in our minds that become our stories, for better or worse, and we do well to understand that these stories are mirrors revealing the truth of who we have become rather than the truth of what has occurred.

The words *humor, humble,* and *human* share a common root meaning "low to the ground." Our most humbling, even humiliating, experiences bring us down, but so do our full-bodied encounters with sheer hilarity. To be human is to be close to the earth, and our memories of the most hilarious and the most humbling moments in our lives can point us toward a great truth.

Take stock now. For this rite, we will create three lists of memories, of moments. Begin with your most hilarious moments; these are times when you were not looking for humor, but there it was. These are sudden encounters with the spontaneous joy of life. Try to recall thirteen moments when you were met with the unbridled humor of being alive, the cosmic joke. Very likely you were not alone in these moments, since humor wants a witness. Notice what other themes come forward from these moments.

Now make a list, a list you are welcome to burn after the rite is over, of thirteen humbling moments. These are the embarrassing times, the sharp moments that often highlight a theme of being misunderstood or something being not quite fair. What patterns do you notice in these achy moments?

Last, make a list of thirteen memories when you felt wholly human. You were fully in the flow of life. You were the most you that you could ever be. What patterns do you notice there?

Do you notice a shared thread between all three lists? You might realize, for example, that there is something very creaturely or uncivilized about many of your thirty-nine memories. You might notice that a particular person is often present, or that a dominant season seems to recur in many of these moments. Consider where and when these moments occurred, and notice if something about your gift's visibility seems tied to these low-to-the-ground times. As we hone our gifts, as we show our genius to the world, we often receive invitations not to take ourselves too seriously. The trick is not to allow the presence of these low-to-the-ground times to keep you from rising and shining.

The shadow side of the mage archetype is similar to the shadow of the wounded healer. The ego swells and takes over, the wound is untended and ignored, and the medicinal power of the archetype is lost, often in favor of fame or fortune. When people who embody these shadow archetypes come into positions of power, the whole world suffers.

Wisdom means understanding, even revering, the power housed inside one's gifts, allowing these gifts to shine and be witnessed while simultaneously keeping low to the ground. Like the students in the Black School who dwelled in the dark for seven years, we are all called to make a home inside the underworld from time to time. We are tasked with regular reflection on what it means to be human, an intensely creative, wildly spiritual animal but an animal nonetheless.

Place three objects on your altar now, if you feel called, one representing what you would call your most hilarious memory, one reflecting back to you your most embarrassing moment, and the last representing your most recent human moment, your in-the-flow-of-life moment.

Rite II: The Genius Spirit in the Bottle

Allow a few days to pass between completing the first rite and beginning this second one. Reflect on any dreams that emerged of late, any signs from nature that seem important. Last, recall your three lists and any common threads between them. In particular, if you consider your human list, what creative actions, what art, is apparent?

You might also ask, When do I feel the boundaries of linear time breaking apart? When do I get lost in a particular action? When have my greatest gifts been witnessed, and how have I amplified my inborn genius, my inner daemon, as the chapters of my life unfold?

As a symbolic action, create now your own genius spirit in a bottle. Gather a bottle or jar that can be sealed with a cork, cap, or lid, along with a piece of paper and writing utensil. On the piece of paper, write what you know to be the gifts you are being called to amplify now. Some of these may already be on your human moment list, but define these golden gifts now. As you do, envision a spirit who fully embodies all you describe, an entity who is the very embodiment of your most shining gifts, a hallowed daemon who illuminates and guards what you have come here to do, that very specific thing that is soul designed.

Roll the list toward you like a scroll, signifying manifestation, then place the list inside the bottle. Speak a prayer or blessing into the vessel and, when you are ready, seal it, placing it on your altar for a time.

Rite III: The Shadow and the Daemon

In the tale of the Black School, Saemunder the Wise does not escape from the underground unscathed. He leaves his shadow there to dwell with the devil in the underworld, a wild metaphor for the deep parts of the psyche. Saemunder's name means "protector of the sea." In Northern European traditions, the sea is the realm of the ancestors and the underworld. The sea is the domain of the deep soul and inherent gifts, the salty cauldron in which the ingredients of our gifts, wounds, joys, griefs, desires, and sorrows all swirl and whirl.

We already know the shadow is what we refuse to see about ourselves, but the shadows are also where our greatest gifts are hidden. When we dare to look at what may lie hidden beneath the parts of us we have refused to love, we see our genius, our daemon, right there behind the iron gate to the underground. The spirit of our genius dwells with our shadow in our psychic underworld, another way of acknowledging that the gift slow-dances with the ache, but we cannot be fully conscious of these parts of ourselves. We are not meant to be; if we were, our life would have no story, no healing quest toward wisdom.

For the final Rite of the Shadow School, go to a place where you can find some dirt. Begin to dig with your hands, and as you do, consider that there are parts of you, parts of your story, that are meant to stay hidden, even from you. We can only see so far, and fate's thread runs through fog and under dark waters. We cannot know exactly where we will go. If we knew the answer to all our questions, we would be dead. To be alive is to live amid secrets, and *secret* means "kept separate." Our soul keeps parts of our story separate, hidden from our view, and that is as it should be.

When the hole feels deep enough, gift your spit to the ground, acknowledge a few of your memories of humor, humbleness, and humanity, and refill the hole with dirt. Press your hands on the ground, and speak a small prayer to the as yet unknown, to the secrets that have yet to be revealed, and to the hidden places.

Eating the Witch's Greens

In the underground shadow schools, we learn we are here to do one very specific thing, but we also learn that we cannot fully understand the nature of that thing. If we did, we might never do it. We might wonder if part of our soul's work before we are born is to choose just what secrets will stay hidden the longest. Perhaps our story is one of small revelations, the slow mining of what was once forbidden, the calling home of our inner exiled children.

Review briefly the Rites of the Shadow School. What do you notice? If there was a part of any rite you chose not to perform, why might that be? Like the parts of a story or dream that feel lost, maybe what you chose not to do can be even more telling than the rituals you did move through. When you feel ready, find a timely threshold, perhaps an iron gate, to cross. After you do, freely speak a prayer that begins: *I have met the spirit of secrets, and now I know...*

We ready ourselves now for our final story here in the Spirit Tower, our last tale from the Night House. Here we eat the witch's greens and sacrifice our long braids. We are exiled twice, once to the tower and once to the wilderness, and we weave together all our lessons from these fate stories.

Chapter 13

◆

The Handmade House

Who is this madwoman? Where is she? Why does she haunt us?
Why do we need to face her now?

LINDA SCHIERSE LEONARD, *Meeting the Madwoman*

The Night House is a hidden place. When we dwell there for a time, we live inside the Yaga's chicken-legged hut, the hag's house of candy, and the woodland tower where the beloved innocent is exiled. In the heart of the house, we hang our wild skin on the wall, warm our hands at the hearth, and listen for the fate stories about shapeshifting women. In the bone cellar, if we dare, we open the red door and hear the bone's song, the stories that speak of the initiatory death and what comes after. Last, here in the spirit tower, we are left with our dreams, with our visions and prayers for the yet-to-come.

Our final story speaks of incubation and the wisdom of solitude. We recall our former lessons here, our experience with the poor bargain's consequences, the father's disrespect of the hag-witch and the daughter's subsequent punishment. We remember the wedding of the wilder self, the role of sacrifice in fulfilling a destiny, and the intelligence of revering our own fate, both what is known and what is yet to be revealed about our personal myth, the story we are living.

This last fate story illuminates those themes and more, for now not only do we return to the haunted woodland; we build a house there

187

with our own hands. We uncover the lost wisdom of the exile, the wanderer, the spiritual initiate who has learned what she can from the witch and now must find her own way forward. As you ready yourself to meet our final Night House fairy tale, reflect on your own moments of exile, of being cast out, shunned like the Thirteenth Wise Woman and left uninvited to the feast. Often these times of abandonment, rejection, and betrayal are what allow the soul to shine. We are locked outside the tower we once called home, forbidden from reentering, and have no choice but to forge our own path through the dark forest.

Invitations for Tale-Tending: Exile in the Wilderness

The walls of our last room in this spirit tower are lined with braided hair, and the ground is a green and growing garden full of forbidden medicine. Here the exiled woman from this story is cast out twice, first from her childhood home and second from the tower where she remained hidden throughout her adolescence. In this story, as before, we want to consider that all the characters are aspects of our own psyche. We are not only the stolen daughter; we are also the ravenous mother, the pitiable father, the wild man, and the hag-witch herself. In the story it is the witch who takes the girl from her home and later casts her out of the tower, so in preparation we ask ourselves to name this inner witch, to see her spirit and welcome her home.

When in your life did your inner witch, that part of you who is always walking with one foot in the Otherworld, pull you from your home? In our story the first exile happens at age twelve, the time of the girl's first blood. The second exile happens as adolescence is ending, as the wild soul encounter approaches. The first exile rips the daughter from her childhood, from the security of her caregivers, while the second disturbs her great plans. The happily-ever-after comes far later than the woman in our story would wish it to, but the second exile had to be, and the witch understood the importance of this rite of passage, this threshold crossing into wiser womanhood. The long braid had to be severed, and the wild house had to be built by the maiden's own hands.

Like Brier Rose, on the surface this story is about a bitter witch who takes revenge on an innocent. Yet underneath we see this is a familiar story lived by many of us who do not wish for a wonder-less life, who allow their inner witch to steal them away from time to time, who find sanctuary in places others do not, the places where the trees bend to the wind's will and the devil dwells in the hollow belly of a dead oak. This story teaches us our final Night House lesson: The new life always demands a sacrifice.

The new life always demands a sacrifice.

To *sacrifice* means "to make sacred." Before meeting our final tale, envision this: a long, severed braid lying on the ground. How do you see this image? What can you say about its nature? What time of day is it, and where do you find this braid? How does this image make you feel? When you are ready, allow the severed braid to speak. What does it tell you? Write down your message from the severed braid. Name it teacher.

Story Altar: The Witch's Rite of Passage

Build this story an altar-house; it deserves one. Include reflections of your most pronounced rites of passage. These are initiatory times when you left home, by your own will or someone else's, faced an incredible ordeal or challenge, and returned from the wilderness as someone new, perhaps someone few recognized. You encountered death, and you lived to tell the tale. Every rite of passage is an initiation, but not every initiation is a rite of passage; these rites are few and far between. We are rendered by them, brought closer to our wilder self. Mark these moments on your altar now. Light a candle for your many old selves, those former lives that were sacrificed so you might live.

The Handmade House

Once upon an autumn moon, an ordinary woman was swollen with a desire to begin again, to leave behind her more innocent ways and welcome the Otherworld into her life. She wanted to mother the wild, you see, and to her that meant birthing a babe who would show her the true meaning of beauty. Night after night, she dreamt of her daughter, fully grown and well-rooted in the world.

The more ravenous she became for her next once-upon-a-time, the more the woman noticed the beauty of the garden beyond her window. A great wall separated her husband's humble farm from the vast and lush expanse. Rumored to belong to an ancient and powerful witch, the garden always glowed with a strange light, and the woman's house was high enough that she could almost see the whole of these magickal grounds that never fallowed. Full of fruit trees, moss, herbs, and every flower imaginable and unimaginable, the witch's garden called to the ordinary woman, enchanting her every morning and seducing her every night. The greater her longing for a child became, the more spellbound by the witch's garden she grew.

Despite all their best efforts, the woman and her husband were unable to conceive a child, and her fantasies about the exquisite garden were the only remedy to her discontent. She'd become lost in daydreams of rolling in the moss, of sinking her teeth into one of the low-hanging pears, and breathing in the heady scent of the golden flowers. More than anything, the woman was full of an overwhelming need to devour the green pillowy leaves that grew closest to the wall, the lamb's lettuce, as her husband called it, but she knew this food by another name, the name her grandmother had used for this healing bounty.

"The greenest rapunzel keeps you young if you eat enough of it," her grandmother said. "Keeps you young, your blood red, and your wits sharp."

Under the full October moon, the ordinary woman was no longer ordinary, for she believed she could hear the green rapunzel singing to her a great song of longing, crying out for her to come and eat. She could hardly sleep, for the rapunzel's song was so loud, and she begged her husband to climb the wall and gather some of the green and growing stuff.

"If I can't have a child, I must have this," she begged, and her husband could hardly refuse her.

It was nearly the day of the dead, and the man put his fears of living corpses and devil goats aside. As midnight approached, the woman watched from her window while her man climbed the wall, falling swiftly into the green leaves she craved with her whole body. Their song grew so loud it was deafening, and her heartbeat pounded while her husband pulled handfuls of the rapunzel up from its roots, stuffing it into his pockets.

In no time at all, he returned to the house, and the woman snarled while she swallowed bite after bite of the only food that would fulfill her desire.

"More," she said after only a few minutes, after she had eaten all her husband had gathered. "I need more."

It was decided the man would return the next night with sacks and baskets, that he would gather up all the rapunzel that grew in the witch's garden. The woman spent the day lost in her imaginings, staring intently at the garden, her belly growling.

That night, as planned, the man climbed the wall with a ring of baskets on his arm and burlap sacks stuffed into his trousers. The woman watched from the window, salivating. She saw the witch before her husband did, and her eyes widened. She held her breath.

"Here for more of my rapunzel, are you?" the old woman hissed, and the man froze. "I'm afraid the punishment for your thievery is death. Now your woman can watch while my pear trees' roots feast on your flesh."

"Wait!" he cried, stepping back. "Surely you have some mercy in your heart. I'm only here because my wife was so hungry. She wishes for a child but, alas, we cannot become pregnant. Your rapunzel was all that could cool her desire."

The witch was quiet for a moment, pensive, then she looked to the window where the woman was watching.

"Very well," she said finally. "I'll let you live. I'll even let you take as much rapunzel as you like as often as you like, but I have one condition."

"Anything," the man promised.

"When your wife becomes pregnant, on the child's twelfth birthday, she is mine."

The man looked to the moon, believing he had no choice in the matter, and agreed to the witch's conditions.

The next day, on the day of the dead, the woman felt sure she was pregnant, and she slept with ease. No more did she crave rapunzel, and her husband told her of the witch's bargain, of the terrible secret.

"We will have twelve years with her, in any case," the woman said after hours of weeping. "Perhaps we can conceive of a plan to hide her before the time comes."

Their daughter was born beautiful, innocent, and free of any care, and the man and woman, peculiar as it was, forgot the fate that was coming for their girl. Every autumn that passed, that night in the witch's garden felt more like a dream. It was too terrible to be true, after all. They even forgot why they had called her Rapunzel, and the woman could scarcely remember who she had been before her babe was born.

Near midnight on Rapunzel's twelfth birthday, the long arms of the witch reached into the girl's window and pulled her from her bed. She carried the sleeping girl to a hidden tower in the haunted forest, a tower that moved every few hours so it could never be found, and the girl remained there for years while her hair grew long and she became a woman, while her mother grieved her loss.

The witch visited Rapunzel daily in the tower, bringing her food and water, teaching her the old ways. Every day at sunrise, the girl would untie her long braids and release them from the window, and the witch, the girl's only company, would climb into the tower. The witch became a stern and sharp-tongued mother to Rapunzel, and the girl missed her true mother's softer ways.

One night as the witching hour neared, Rapunzel found she could not sleep. She looked out at the full Blood Moon, and her eyes fell on a wild man riding a dark horse through the woodland. She was taken with him, thinking he might be a ghost, but did not call out. That night she dreamt they were wed.

The next day, after the witch's daily visit, Rapunzel stared from the window and began singing a song of longing, a deep and guttural song that shook the trees and rode the West wind straight to the wild man's ears. Consumed by this song, he followed the sound and, as dusk fell, he found the tower and its golden-haired prisoner.

"My lady," he called, and she stopped her song. "May I come up?"

Remembering her dream, she shunned all the witch's warnings

about strangers and let her long braids fall. He climbed and climbed, and Rapunzel was full of heat for him. When he reached the window, she welcomed him, poured him some of the witch's wine, and told him her story. All night the wild man stayed, but as the fog lightened in the forest around them, they knew dawn was coming.

"The witch will be here soon," Rapunzel said. "You must go."

"I'll return at sunset," the wild man vowed, and he climbed down her long braids.

As autumn turned to winter, their romance continued. Every dusk, the wild man climbed into the tower. They would spend the night together, falling deeper and deeper in love, and every dawn, he would leave before the witch could catch them together.

"I must be free of this place," Rapunzel whispered one night as she lay in the wild man's arms. "But I cannot climb down my own hair, I fear."

They hatched a plan then. Every night when the wild man came to visit, he would bring a single strand of silk from which Rapunzel would slowly weave a ladder. As winter turned to spring, the ladder took form, the witch was none the wiser, and the two lovers believed their escape was imminent.

Rapunzel grew bolder with every passing day, and for the first time she was full of rage at the witch who had stolen her from her parents, from her simple, joyful life. It was nearly summer now, and the forest was lush and beautiful. She hated being locked in the tower and longed to see her wild man in the daylight.

On the morning of the longest day, while the witch climbed her hair, Rapunzel was ireful.

"Why does my wild man weigh less than you, witch?" she spit, and the old woman's eyes widened as she climbed inside the window.

"What did you say?"

Rapunzel said nothing, knowing she had made a grave mistake.

"You forget who I am," the witch hissed, and she grabbed Rapunzel's braids and severed them with her blade. Before she knew it, Rapunzel was suddenly alone and in a harsh land. The stones were sharp here, and the wolves howled in the distance. Her bald head was bleeding, and she fell to her knees and wept.

Meanwhile, the witch waited in the tower for the wild man to arrive, throwing down the severed braids at dusk so he could climb up and meet his fate.

"Your little bird is not here," the witch hissed when he climbed through the window, and the wild man was broken by his grief. He saw the blood on the braids and believed his love to be dead. In his sorrow, he threw himself from the tower, hoping for death.

When he woke from his fall, he found he was still breathing but could not see. He had fallen on thorns that had poked his eyes, and his horse had left him. While the full Blood Moon rose, he began his great wander through the woodland, an aimless journey that lasted many years.

Rapunzel, alone in the harsh land, found she was pregnant as the nights grew longer and colder. She built a house with her own hands on the rocks. She kept her hair short, and she learned how to live on the untamed ground. There, in the rough place, she raised her twin babes.

One year, close to the first harvest day in early August, when her twins were nearly twelve years old, though she hadn't sung the song of longing in many years, she felt the sound swelling deep within her body.

All day long she sang, and as the sun began to sink low into the mountain, a shadow approached. She kept singing, and the shadow kept coming, and just as the sun disappeared, she saw the face of her wild man.

"Is it you?" he whispered, unable to see her.

"Yes. Yes, it's me," she wept, and her tears fell into his marred eyes, making them whole again. He could suddenly see her and his children, having wandered so long through the dark forest, and the four of them lived happily ever after, made so, as we all are, by gratitude and grief.

The Three Rites of the Exile

Our story begins with hunger, with a woman's ravenous desire to become someone new, to be a mother. Our story ends with a wild woman who built her own house in a rough place, who also became someone new after a brutal initiation. The shaving of one's hair, the severing of the braids, has always been a symbol of initiation, of grief, of renunciation. Cutting a woman's hair and sending her into the wilderness is an ancient and archetypal act; though we may not have experienced this literally in our lives, even so we understand it. Somehow we remember this exile. We know this story.

In our tale Rapunzel is very like Lilith, the first wife of Adam, who was cast out of Eden for her willful behavior, her refusal to be subservient. Rapunzel's time in the tower is finished, her education complete, and now her path is her own. Her old self is destroyed, and she has no choice but to seek her new name, her ultimate liberation as an exile from all she once knew.

Now that our story has ended, name your one remaining question. Does it feel like any part of the plot is missing? Do you have a small wonder — or a big one? Write this question down. For the last time, ask yourself, How is my question about this fairy tale the very question of my life right now? Name the question an oracle. Why is this your question? What does the question illuminate about a life area that is in transition right now? Reshape the question slightly to be a question about your life. Let the question become more personal.

Recall your message from the severed braid. How is this message an answer to your question? Let this be a new beginning somehow, this question-and-answer pairing. Notice what is revealed and what remains hidden by this question and answer, and then begin these last rites, the Rites of the Exile.

Rite I: The Hunger

We have already considered the potency of a name, the vows and small stories contained within the names we chose for ourselves and the names we were given. In the story of Brier Rose, she is named after the specific wildflowers that will protect her, that will shield her while she sleeps the long sleep. In this story the maiden is named after the wild growing greens that her mother craved and her father stole. If it is a worthy inquiry for you, you might ask if there is something your mother or another caregiver craved that is hidden in your name. We also cannot know for sure, of course, whether another intelligence was afoot when our names were decided. Perhaps the spirit of the child was already there, calling her mother, causing the craving.

When we consider our desires, those witch's wants we might cast a spell for, if we feel so inclined, we want to sense those powerful longings that seem to call us toward them, that want us as much as we want them. If there is such thing as a best fate, an optimal path on which we can orient ourselves, then maybe the wants that call us toward them are showing us how to find this path. If fate limits us and destiny liberates us, then maybe, just maybe, there are autonomous destiny choices we make within the confines of our fate, within the container of our story, that will allow the best fate to unfold.

For our first Rite of the Exile, go for a solitary wander. If you are able, carry little or nothing with you. If you can do so safely, leave your phone at home. As a symbolic action, you might also leave behind something that is almost always with you, a ring or another piece of jewelry, perhaps. Shed something, like the shedding of hair, and go into nature.

Walk slowly. Ponder the desire that longs for you as much as you long for it. Let this moment feel both fated and chosen. Perhaps all your work in the Night House has been leading to this knowing. Like the mother and daughter in our story, you might begin to sing the song of longing, whatever that means to you. Walk until you can define this thing you hunger for so wildly. Let it surprise you. Let it sting you awake.

Notice how the clouds move, how the weather and creatures sing with you. Hear them. When you feel ready, only when you feel somehow changed, speak a prayer of gratitude. Find stillness. Look for a sign, a nod from nature that tells you this rite is finished, and then return home.

Rite II: The Witch's Ladder

Reflect on your experience with the first rite, and notice if it brought about any clarity. If time has passed since the completion of the first rite, briefly notice any strange synchronicities that found you. For our second rite, you will need three lengths of fabric, string, or ribbon. One of these pieces will reflect that particular hunger you named during the first rite's wild wander. Another of these pieces will reflect fate, your soul's lot, and the last piece will represent destiny, your most liberating and soul-fulfilling path. Let these lengths of fabric, string, or ribbon be about three feet or one meter long. Their width does not matter. Choose pieces that feel representative of those three ideas, however — your hunger, your fate, and your destiny.

In our story we have the ladder of hair that allows both the witch and the wild man to climb into the tower. This is the same ladder, of course, that is destroyed at the beginning of the woman's last exile, when she was cast into the wilderness. Initiation always begins with severance, after all. The ladder is severed, and the old way is broken. The two lovers try to weave their own ladder, their own way, with the wild man bringing the material slowly while the maiden weaves, but their task is stunted, left incomplete by the witch's discovery of their secret.

Witch's ladders, a form of old Celtic folk magick, are generally used for protection, healing, or manifestation. In our second rite, our witch's ladder will be a ladder of manifestation, a symbolic weaving of fate, destiny, and our witch's want. When you are ready, hold the ends of all three pieces together, and tie your first knot.

Reflect on those storytelling weaver-women, hidden away in the spinning rooms, exiles in their own right. Reflect on your own weaver-women ancestors, the knitters and the seamstresses. When you are ready, anchor the knot you just made under something heavy. You can also hold it down with your foot, if you choose. Begin to slowly and mindfully braid the three pieces. Take your time. Find a rhythm. As you braid, consider that thing called fate and what these Night House stories have shown you about your own living fairy tale. Think of your own severed braids, the sacrifices and the shed skins. Think of the many crossroads of your life, the choices that liberated you, that set you on a new path that you now know was the healing path, the right road for you to walk. Last, tend to that hunger. Hone that vision, that witch's want. Keep braiding. Every three or four inches, make a knot, then keep braiding.

Your complete ladder will have thirteen knots total, including the first knot you made, with braiding in between. As you work you might sing the song of longing that emerged during the first rite. Let the song be like a charm. Let it travel. Let it infuse your work. When the ladder feels finished, bless it with your breath, and place it on your altar until you are ready to move on to our final rite.

Rite III: The Handmade House

As our story nears its end, the braid lies bloody on the floor. The old way is broken. The wild man is blind and wandering, and the exiled woman builds her own house in the wilderness. Her last house, her third house, is neither the home from her childhood nor the tower where she was locked during her adolescence. This new place, built by her own hands, is an uncivilized place built on untamed ground, a pagan place where her wild children can live.

In the old stories the third time is indeed the charm, as we know. This third house is the woman's handmade home, hard-won and built in solitude while her belly was heavy with new life. We don't know exactly how she did it, and we don't need to. The ending of this story is familiar nonetheless. The hardest thing we do in our lives may, to those on the outside looking in, appear easy, but we remember the sweat and the sleeplessness and the terror. We remember the labor of it and how that labor fits inside our larger story.

You might recall moments from childhood when you created your own home, a tiny dwelling that was just yours. The weeping willow branches were the swaying walls of a sanctuary, or a quilt draped just so over kitchen chairs became your castle. We have been building the Night House our whole lives.

For our final rite, go into the wilds, and carry your witch's ladder. Find a place you can call yours for a time, a hidden place where you can wear your wild skin and be your most uncivilized self. Face the direction that feels like home once you are there. Breathe.

Recall now all our stories from the Night House. Remember little Red Hood and her liberation from the wolf's belly. Remember the Coat of Moss, the feathery pelt worn by the Swan Maiden, and the tattered old hood. Call to mind the singing bone, the warrior bird-woman, the Girl of the Moon, the Ash Fool's chant to the hazelwood, and the shapeshifting Blackbird Boy. Remember Brier Rose and the

Thirteenth Wise Woman. Remember the ruined one's dream, the Spirit in the Bottle, and the devil's underground schoolhouse. Think of Rapunzel's story, from her mother's hunger to her tower training, from falling for the wild man and yet again becoming outcast. Now, like her, build your own house here in this wilderness.

Invite guests from our stories. Who is welcome here? Call them forward, along with those long-gone storytelling ancestors. Stay here for a time. Speak a small story out loud for your guests to witness. Mark this moment. Let it become great. Tend to the spirit of this, your symbolic homecoming. If it feels right, hang your witch's ladder here when you are ready. Leave it as a prayer bundle, as a memory, as a healing act. Stay here for as long as you like, knowing you can return whenever you wish, but — and this is important — when you do leave, when you cross that imagined threshold between this and that, speak a small prayer that begins with these words: *I have visited the Night House, and now I know...*

And It All Ends to Begin Again

The old stories never really end, we know. The ever-after is always followed by a once-upon-a-time. It all ends to begin again.

As you leave the Night House, offer a gift to the hag who tends this old place. Know you can return here whenever you need to, whenever life gets too ordinary. Take to the otherworldly road when you feel caught in the mundane, when you wake without enchantment and wish you could remember where you hid your wild skin.

A story can save or destroy a whole world. When you begin tending stories, you see them everywhere. You see the politician's blue beard and the musician's feathered pelt. You wonder what character you play in the world story, and how you can best bewitch the world from the inside out.

Stay curious about the power of story. Let these tales live on your tongue. Be story-keeper and tale-tender, and watch your world transform in the space between a *once* and an *after*.

LESSONS FROM THE SPIRIT TOWER

What we do inside fate's house is up to us.

Dreams illuminate the yet-to-come.

Each of us is here to heal one specific thing.

The new life always demands a sacrifice.

Conclusion

Closing the Red Door

The red door to the Night House is closed, and we left the hag sleeping. A red sun is rising behind the tangled silhouettes of the oaks and the hazels, and we must return to the homeward road. Come with me, and meet one final story as we journey back to the day house. Let me tell you of the cunning woman who saved the world by telling 1,001 stories.

The Scheherazade

Once in a time long gone and still here, there lived a wealthy sultan who relished his power. While he found he could wield his power over much of his kingdom, there was one great creature that seemed beyond his control, a force of nature that, try as he might, the sultan could never tame.

"Women," he would hiss, clicking his tongue in disgust.

When the sultan was young, he'd come home from a hunting trip to find his wife in bed with another man. Reeling with madness, he killed her, and then traveled to his brother's house in hope of finding comfort with family. When he arrived there, his brother was not home, but his brother's wife was indulging in pleasures of the flesh that shocked and tormented him. In a fit of rage, he made the unthinkable the law of the land.

Every night, he would take a virgin to his bed, and the next morning at dawn, he would have her beheaded so she could not betray him.

Word of the sultan's horrors spread, and families began to leave the kingdom in fear of their daughters' fates. More terrible laws were enacted, and women found they could no longer thrive in their ancestral lands.

"We must go at once," a good father said to his dear daughter Scheherazade and her sister one evening. "It is not safe for you here."

Unlike every other woman in the kingdom, Scheherazade refused to leave.

"No, Father. Let me stay and marry this sultan," she said, and in time it was so. Scheherazade became the sultan's new bride, and everyone assumed the poor woman would meet the same fate as those who came before her.

On her wedding night, Scheherazade asked the sultan if she could see her sister one last time and, as they had arranged, the sister asked Scheherazade to tell her a story.

That night Scheherazade spun the wildest tale, and the sultan was captivated by her and her storytelling. She ended the story by beginning another, a sudden twist in the plot spilling from her tongue as the sun rose, and the sultan could not kill her; if he did, he would never find out what happened next in the story.

This went on, as they say, for 1,001 nights. Each night, Scheherazade would spill lost stories from her lips, as if they were channeled straight from the Otherworld, but she would always end the night by beginning a new story. Slowly, surely, over nearly three years' time, the sultan fell deeply in love with Scheherazade.

When the last story was told, he repented his wickedness, and the true love affair between the sultan and his famed storytelling wife began.

As the World Turns and Churns

A good storyteller understands the power of a tale's opening words. *Once upon a time* is a blade that slices through the hours, that cracks open our best notions about linear time, and opens a wide mouth the audience falls into. *Once upon a time, back in the days when animals could speak, in a time long gone, say the old ones…* These fairy tale beginnings give us the shock of the strange, their language just peculiar enough to open the red door between the real and the imagined, between the possible and the impossible, the human and Other, then and now.

When we share the old stories, we are tapping into the oral traditions of our foremothers, who wielded story in the best possible way: to subvert the systems that bound them. As the world turns and churns, storytelling remains a formidable tool for social change, personal growth, and radical transformation. Whole plans for disruption are hidden inside a story; we need only to let the old stories breathe, reanimating them for our time and mining the medicine from the lost underground libraries.

A good story can trick a king, wrecking the sultan's terrible reign and rocking the very foundations of crumbling systems. The name Scheherazade means "noble lineage," and she, that great and wild storyteller, was setting right a wrong in the name of her foremothers, sisters, and unborn daughters, in the name of the common people. When she spoke the word *once*, she cracked open the ruler's world every night, charming him into submission with tales of wonder and enchantment, softening him to his own shadow's intelligence, inviting him to consider the worth of innocence, his own legacy, and perhaps the whispered wisdoms of his own ancestors. Her *once* was a spoken charm, a spell that bewitched that ruler and lured him into her Night House, an oracle disguised as a bedtime story that illuminated possibilities he would not have seen otherwise.

A story disturbs the water. A story stirs the pot. Our task as tale-tenders is to let the story live and breathe, but we cannot get caught in its belly. We cannot stay in any story for too long, lest we are blinded to our next once-upon-a-time. The red door must close. Stories are meant to end so a new one can begin; the dawn always comes. We leave the Night House so we can bring the healing stories into the light, carrying the medicine we uncovered there back to our ancestors, back to the grandmother's house.

The rooms you visited in the Night House, in these pages, are an invitation to become a tale-tender. *To initiate* means "to begin," after all, so begin now. Initiate the new story. Tell a tale that troubles the systems in your world that you would like to see fall, that wakes the very beast that will swallow the outmoded structures whole, that dismantles the old beliefs and burns their house to the ground, that bewitches the kings to lay down their swords and amplifies the sound of the bone's song. Bring others to the Night House. Now you know the way.

I'll leave you here as the stars fade, as the new day comes for us all. May we live well now and ever after.

And so it is.

Appendix

------✦------

Night House Practices

Courting a Story:
Relationship Tips for the Tale-Tender

There is no correct, academic process for storytelling, no award to be won, achievement to unlock, or uppermost tier to reach. If you wish to tell an old story well, you might just let it seduce you. Remember every story is, in part, a love story. Ask, What do I love most about this world? Find a story that amplifies *that*.

A tale-tender is a loyal lover. They hold a fierce loyalty to the story and would never dare betray its heart. A tale-tender makes room for their relationship with the story to live and breathe. Like twin flames encircled in a heated love affair, the story and the storyteller change each other slowly, surely. When a story invites you in, tries to claim you for its own, you might just dare to dance with it for a time, to let it whisper against your skin and find you in the dreaming time. When this happens, here are a few relationship tips:

1. When an old story returns for you, read as many different versions as you can. Dig into the dusty corners of antique stores and questionable virtual back rooms. Watch the polished film version and study the local lore surrounding the story. Take time to understand where it comes from and who it has encountered during its time.

2. Consider what single image from the story seems the most enchanting, the most seductive. Go into nature and find an object — a mossy stone or a reddening leaf, anything that calls out to you — that reflects that story image back to you.

3. Build an altar to the story centering that object. As we did with our Night House stories, open and tend a physical place for the tale to live in your house, in your garden, somewhere close.

4. Notice how the imagery from the story shows up for you in your everyday experience, in the memories that surface and the dreams that come. Notice how the story's spirit reaches out to you.

5. When you feel ready, speak the story out loud from the once to the after. Be witnessed, if only by your ghosts. Let the Otherworld speak through you. Notice the words you speak that surprise you, the story's happenings you seem to amplify through your voice, your gestures. Let the story have its way with you. Surrender to its rhythm. Take your time, and let it live and breathe through you.

The Night House Oracle

If you feel called, if you were struck by the imagery in these stories, consider creating a spontaneous oracle deck that reflects the messages you received. Review your notes from the tale-tending sections of this book, where you met an image from the coming story and named it teacher. Gather any art materials you wish, along with blank, unlined index cards. At the top of each card, write the name of the fairy tale symbol — the haunted woodland or the severed braid, for instance — then at the bottom of the card, write your message from that image. At the center of the card, you might draw this image as you see it now.

Last, on the back of each card, draw a simple symbol that is the same on every card; this might be a pentagram, a heart, a red door, a spiral, or a sigil you create. Here is a list of the thirteen symbols from our stories, but feel free to add others. Feel free to let your dream symbols and visions participate. Make use of this deck as you would any other oracle, carrying your questions to it, pulling a single card when guidance is needed, scripting a new story for yourself, your people, and the world.

1. The haunted woodland
2. The coat of moss
3. The feathered pelt
4. The tattered hood
5. The singing bone
6. The wild egg
7. The dark moon
8. The spirit tree
9. The crow
10. The spinning wheel
11. The ruined house
12. The shadow
13. The severed braid

The Fairy-Tale Council

Choose a fairy tale to work with for this practice that houses a villainous shadow for you. This is a fairy-tale villain to whom you have a visceral reaction. If you're able, read a few different versions of this story. Build a small altar to it. Let it brew for at least two weeks, ideally while the moon is waning.

When you're ready, make a list of all the important characters in this story, naming only those you feel are essential to the tale. You might also name magickal objects or the seductive settings as characters. Try to get at least five, but you can have many more. If you are working with the Mage's Bird story, for instance, you might name the warrior bird-woman, the wild egg, the mage's basket, the blue-bearded mage himself, and the red door. Let these characters and images sit in council with you for a time.

Ideally when the moon is new, bring a particular problem or source of conflict in your life to this fairy-tale council. Imagine you are seated around a table with these story spirits. Grant them mythic names if they don't already have them. Out loud in the "heart voice," a whisper, tell the council about the source of conflict or problem. It can be vague or specific. Express to the council what you'd like them to know.

Then — and this is about to get stranger — begin to embody each character, each image, one at a time, allowing the character to gift you their wisdom about your particular problem. Let each character re-source you. What would the Swan Maiden or the lonely hunter tell you? Channel the fairy-tale wisdom, and write down the important words or phrases each character says.

You might do this with many stories or just one. In reflection, ask, Which characters did I feel a peculiar kinship with? Why might that be? What else did I notice about this practice?

Acknowledgments

To my beloved wild suns, Bodhi and Sage, thank you for choosing me as your mother, for shining so brilliantly even when the world is full of shadow. To my bread-baking, land-tending, and open-hearted husband, Ryan, thank you for cooking for the witches who visit our haunted land, for feeding me and loving me so well. To those I have been blessed to call teacher — Bayo Akomolafe, Dr. Clarissa Pinkola Estés, John Cantwell, and Dr. Karen Ward — thank you for your immense wisdom, your writings, and your sacred work in the world. To the team at New World Library, including my editor Georgia Hughes and publicist Kim Corbin, and to my agents Sheree Bykofsky and Jill Marsal, the deepest bows and wildest howls for all the work you have done in midwifing these strange books of mine. To my grandmothers, Grace and Mary, thank you for your wisdom, for continuing to live through me and my children, even and especially now.

Notes

Introduction

p. 3   *Fairy tales were never intended*: Jack Zipes, *The Irresistible Fairy Tale* (Princeton University Press, 2012), 20.

p. 4   *Others say they were teaching tales*: Marie-Louise von Franz, *Shadow and Evil in Fairy Tales* (Shambhala, 1995), 11.

p. 4   *What distinguishes a fairy tale*: Marina Warner, *From the Beast to the Blonde: On Fairy Tales and Their Tellers* (Farrar, Straus & Giroux, 1994), xxi.

p. 5   *"until about the seventeenth century"*: Von Franz, *Shadow and Evil*, 10.

p. 8   *If we mine the original meaning*: Online Etymology Dictionary, "rite," last updated September 3, 2021, https://www.etymonline.com/word/rite.

p. 8   *We encounter our unique soul's truth*: Michael Meade, *Fate and Destiny: The Two Agreements of the Soul* (Greenfire, 2012), 142.

p. 9   *Many of the more famous male story collectors*: Julie Koehler et al., eds., *Women Writing Wonder: An Anthology of Subversive Nineteenth-Century British, French, and German Fairy Tales* (Wayne State University Press, 2021), 30, 198.

Chapter 1: The Red Hood

p. 13   *"In a well-honed crone"*: Marion Woodman and Elinor Dickson, *Dancing in the Flames: The Dark Goddess in the Transformation of Consciousness* (Shambhala, 1997), 10.

p. 16   *Once in a time that was remembered*: Based on "Little Red Cap," collected by Jacob and Wilhelm Grimm from Jeanette and Marie Hassenpflug, "Rothkäppchen," in *Kinder- und Hausmärchen gesammelt durch die Brüder Grimm*,

1st ed., trans. D. L. Ashliman, vol. 1, no. 26 (Realschulbuchhandlung, 1812), 113–18, available at https://sites.pitt.edu/~dash/type0333.html.

p. 20   *In a traditional indigenous rite of passage*: Malidoma Somé, "Between Two Worlds: Malidoma Somé on Rites of Passage," interview by Leslee Goodman, *The Sun*, no. 415 (July 2010), available at https://ifnatural learning.com/resources/540-2.

p. 21   *Following the severance is the void*: For more insight on the initiation process, see Robert Moore, *The Archetype of Initiation: Sacred Space, Ritual Process, and Personal Transformation: Lectures and Essays*, ed. Max J. Havlick Jr. (Xlibris, 2001).

p. 21   *These initiatory stages have been reframed*: For a description of the feminine initiation process, see Ronald Grimes, *Deeply into the Bone: Re-Inventing Rites of Passage* (University of California Press, 2002).

p. 22   *Only after believing they would die*: Somé, "Between Two Worlds."

p. 23   *"Typical meeting places for women alone"*: Marina Warner, *From the Beast to the Blonde: On Fairy Tales and Their Tellers* (Farrar, Straus & Giroux, 1994), 35.

Chapter 2: The Coat of Moss

p. 27   *"Let your craft be rooted in the words"*: Roger J. Horne, *The Witch's Art of Incantation: Spoken Charms, Spells & Curses in Folk Witchcraft* (Moon Over the Mountain, 2023), 40.

p. 27   *The term* fairy tale *was not used*: Nicholas Jubber, *The Fairy Tellers* (Nicholas Brealey, 2022), 4.

p. 27   *The etymology of the word* fairy: Marina Warner, *From the Beast to the Blonde: On Fairy Tales and Their Tellers* (Farrar, Straus & Giroux, 1994), 14–15.

p. 28   *The word* gossip *originally referred*: Warner, *From the Beast*, 14–15.

p. 28   *A witch is someone who holds*: Online Etymology Dictionary, "Wicca," last updated August 19, 2018, https://www.etymonline.com/word/Wicca.

p. 30   *Once in a time that was always*: Based on "Mossy Coat," a Romani story collected by T. W. Thompson from Taimi Boswell in 1915, in Katharine Mary Briggs and Ruth L. Tongue, eds., *Folktales of England* (University of Chicago Press, 1965), 16.

p. 40   *In the end, though, you know that*: Online Etymology Dictionary, "purpose," last updated March 25, 2024, https://www.etymonline.com/word/purpose.

Chapter 3: The Swan Maiden

p. 43   *"In human lives, stories precede"*: Arthur W. Frank, *Letting Stories Breathe: A Socio-Narratology* (University of Chicago Press, 2010), 46.

Notes

p. 44   *"Mother Stork's part in storytelling"*: Marina Warner, *From the Beast to the Blonde: On Fairy Tales and Their Tellers* (Farrar, Straus & Giroux, 1994), 64.

p. 46   *"Emblematic signs of the goose"*: Warner, *From the Beast*, 65.

p. 46   *Once upon a full Blood Moon*: Based on "The Swan Maiden," in Herman Hofberg, *Swedish Fairy Tales*, trans. W. H. Myers (Belford-Clarke, 1890), 35–38, available at https://sites.pitt.edu/~dash/swan.html.

p. 52   *When we consider our inner shadows*: See Bill Plotkin, *Wild Mind: A Field Guide to the Human Psyche* (New World Library, 2013) for more information on the shadow.

Chapter 4: The Shadow Twin

p. 53   *"If one lived quite alone"*: Marie-Louise von Franz, *Shadow and Evil in Fairy Tales* (Shambhala, 1995), 7.

p. 56   *Once in a time that was and was not*: Based on Peter Christen Asbjørnsen and Jørgen Moe, "Tatterhood" ("Lurvehette"), in *Norske folkeeventyr* (1842–1852), trans. George Webb Dasent (1859), translation revised by D. L. Ashliman (2001), available at https://sites.pitt.edu/~dash/norway122.html.

p. 66   *In* Women Who Run with the Wolves: Clarissa Pinkola Estés, *Women Who Run with the Wolves: Myths and Stories of the Wild Woman Archetype* (Ballantine, 1992), 71.

p. 67   *Anodea Judith describes*: Anodea Judith, *Eastern Body, Western Mind: Psychology and the Chakra System as a Path to the Self* (Celestial Arts, 1996), 118.

Chapter 5: The Bone's Song

p. 75   *"We all begin as a bundle of bones"*: Clarissa Pinkola Estés, *Women Who Run with the Wolves: Myths and Stories of the Wild Woman Archetype* (Ballantine, 1992), 26.

p. 77   *Once in a time that is forever gone*: Based on "The Singing Bone," collected by Jacob and Wilhelm Grimm, "Der singende Knochen," in *Kinder- und Hausmärchen gesammelt durch die Brüder Grimm*, trans. D. L. Ashliman, vol. 1, no. 28 (Realschulbuchhandlung, 1812), available at https://sites.pitt.edu/~dash/grimm028.html.

p. 83   *The shepherd is the inner caregiver*: Carol Pearson, *What Stories Are You Living?: Discover Your Archetypes — Transform Your Life!* (Center for Applications of Psychological Type, 2021), 47.

p. 85   *"part of the miracle of the wild psyche"*: Estés, *Women Who Run*, 410.

Chapter 6: The Mage's Bird

p. 87 *"In a sense, we are servants"*: Michael Meade, *Fate and Destiny: The Two Agreements of the Soul* (Greenfire, 2012), 232.

p. 90 *Once in a time that came and went*: Based on "Fitcher's Bird," collected by Jacob and Wilhelm Grimm from Friederike Mannel (1783–1833) and Henriette Dorothea (Dortchen) Wild (1795–1867), "Fitchers Vogel," in *Kinder- und Hausmärchen gesammelt durch die Brüder Grimm*, 7th ed., trans. D. L. Ashliman, vol. 1, no. 46 (Verlag der Dieterichschen Buchhandlung, 1857), 228–31, available at https://sites.pitt.edu/~dash /grimm046.html.

p. 98 Apocalypse *means revelation*: *Online Etymology Dictionary*, "apocalypse," last updated March 13, 2023, https://www.etymonline.com/word /apocalypse.

p. 99 *The trickster cannot be trusted*: Lewis Hyde, *Trickster Makes This World: Mischief, Myth, and Art* (Farrar, Straus & Giroux, 1998), 6–7.

p. 100 *Birds were associated with birth*: See Marina Warner, *From the Beast to the Blonde: On Fairy Tales and Their Tellers* (Farrar, Straus & Giroux, 1994), 51–65 for more on the associations between birds, women, and fairy tales.

Chapter 7: The Skull Groom

p. 103 *"The English word 'hell'"*: Demetra George, *Mysteries of the Dark Moon: The Healing Power of the Dark Goddess* (HarperCollins, 1992), 35.

p. 103 *Our creaturely brains see*: For more insight on the human brain and psychic ability, see Serena Roney-Dougal, *Where Science and Magic Meet* (Green Magic, 2010).

p. 104 *In* From the Beast to the Blonde: Marina Warner, *From the Beast to the Blonde: On Fairy Tales and Their Tellers* (Farrar, Straus & Giroux, 1994), 51–65.

p. 105 *In* Mysteries of the Dark Moon: George, *Mysteries*, 19–20.

p. 105 *In an old Irish folk tale*: Collected from Maureen Clery, Árd Phádraig, The Irish Folklore Commission Collection, University College Dublin, available at https://www.duchas.ie/en/cbes/4922041/4921307.

p. 107 *Once, never, and always*: Based on "The Disobedient Daughter Who Married a Skull," in Elphinstone Dayrell, *Folk Stories from Southern Nigeria, West Africa*, no. 8 (Longmans, Green, 1910), 38–41, available at https://sites.pitt.edu/~dash//skull.html.

p. 109 *In* Caliban and the Witch: See Silvia Federici, *Caliban and the Witch: Women, the Body, and Primitive Accumulation* (Autonomedia, 2004).

Notes

Chapter 8: The Ash Fool

p. 115 *"In fairy tales, as in life"*: Bruno Bettelheim, *The Uses of Enchantment: The Meaning and Importance of Fairy Tales* (Random House, 2010), 9.

p. 117 *In a time long, long gone and about to be*: Based on "The Ash Fool," collected by Jacob and Wilhelm Grimm, "Aschenputtel," in *Kinder- und Hausmärchen gesammelt durch die Brüder Grimm*, 1st ed., trans. D. L. Ashliman, vol. 1, no. 21 (Realschulbuchhandlung, 1812), available at https://sites.pitt.edu/~dash/grimm021.html.

p. 126 *"In the natural process of maturing"*: Clarissa Pinkola Estés, *Women Who Run with the Wolves: Myths and Stories of the Wild Woman Archetype* (Ballantine, 1992), 84.

p. 127 *A charm in witchcraft*: Roger J. Horne, *The Witch's Art of Incantation: Spoken Charms, Spells & Curses in Folk Witchcraft* (Moon Over the Mountain, 2023), 30.

Chapter 9: The Blackbird Boy

p. 133 *"Grief has a sound"*: Martín Prechtel, *The Smell of Rain on Dust: Grief and Praise* (North Atlantic, 2015), 5.

p. 135 *Once in a time full of sages and fools*: Based on "The Bewitched Brothers," in M. Gaster, *Rumanian Bird and Beast Stories*, no. 77 (Folk-Lore Society, 1915), 231–35, available at https://sites.pitt.edu/~dash/type0451.html.

p. 139 *In the old story "The Handless Maiden"*: Based on "The Girl Without Hands," collected by Jacob and Wilhelm Grimm from Marie Hassenpflug, "Das Mädchen ohne Hände," in *Kinder- und Hausmärchen gesammelt durch die Brüder Grimm*, 7th ed., trans. D. L. Ashliman, vol. 1, no. 31 (Verlag der Dieterichschen Buchhandlung, 1857), 162–68, available at https://sites.pitt.edu/~dash/grimm031.html.

Chapter 10: The Thirteenth Wise Woman

p. 145 *"And one day, just a moment ago"*: Martin Shaw, *Scatterlings: Getting Claimed in the Age of Amnesia* (White Cloud, 2018), 17–18.

p. 146 *She is the elder feminine made manifest*: Gearóid Ó Crualaoich, *Book of the Cailleach: Stories of the Wise-Woman Healer* (Cork University Press, 2006).

p. 147 *Fate, they say, is family*: For more insight on the relationship between fate and family, see Michael Meade, *Fate and Destiny: The Two Agreements of the Soul* (Greenfire, 2012).

p. 148 *Once alive and then dead and now alive again*: Based on "Little Brier-Rose," collected by Jacob and Wilhelm Grimm from Marie Hassenpflug,

"Dornröschen," in *Kinder- und Hausmärchen gesammelt durch die Brüder Grimm*, 7th ed., trans. D. L. Ashliman, vol. 1, no. 50 (Verlag der Dieterichschen Buchhandlung, 1857), 252–54, available at https://sites.pitt.edu/~dash/grimm050.html.

p. 158   *What if these dreams were sent to us*: For more information on precognitive dreaming, see Eric Wargo, *Time Loops: Precognition, Retrocausation, and the Unconscious* (Anomalist Books, 2018).

Chapter 11: The Ruined One's Dream

p. 161   *"We are on the cusp of a revolution"*: Eric Wargo, *Precognitive Dreamwork and the Long Self: Interpreting Messages from Your Future* (Inner Traditions, 2021), 269.

p. 163   weird *comes from* wyrd: *Online Etymology Dictionary*, "weird," last updated November 10, 2022, https://www.etymonline.com/word/weird #etymonline_v_4898.

p. 163   *"future towers out of past bricks"*: Wargo, *Precognitive Dreamwork*, 68.

p. 164   *Once in a time gone, gone*: Based on "The Ruined Man Who Became Rich Again Through a Dream," in *The Book of the Thousand Nights and a Night*, trans. John Payne, vol. 4 (printed for subscribers only, 1884), 134–35, available at https://sites.pitt.edu/~dash/type1645.html.

Chapter 12: The Devil's School

p. 173   *"Where you have a mythic image"*: Joseph Campbell, *Pathways to Bliss: Mythology and Personal Transformation* (New World Library, 2004), xvi.

p. 174   demon *stems from* daemon, *which means "genius"*: *Online Etymology Dictionary*, "demon," last updated October 13, 2021, https://www.etym online.com/word/demon#etymonline_v_5575.

p. 175   *Once in a time that was known and unknown*: Based on "The Spirit in the Bottle," collected by Jacob and Wilhelm Grimm from an unnamed tailor, "Der Geist im Glas," in *Kinder- und Hausmärchen gesammelt durch die Brüder Grimm*, trans. D. L. Ashliman, vol. 2, no. 9 (numbered 99 in more recent editions) (1815), available at https://sites.pitt.edu /~dash/grimm099.html.

p. 179   *Once and still, a dark dwelling*: Based on "The Black School," in Jón Árnason, *Icelandic Legends*, trans. George E. J. Powell and Eiríkur Magnússon (Richard Bentley, 1864), 226–28, available at https://sites.pitt.edu/~dash /type3000.html.

p. 181   *The word* reflection *means*: *Online Etymology Dictionary*, "reflection," last updated June 10, 2021, https://www.etymonline.com/word/reflection #etymonline_v_10293.

p. 184 secret *means "kept separate"*: *Online Etymology Dictionary*, "secret," last updated April 15, 2022, https://www.etymonline.com/word/secret #etymonline_v_23083.

Chapter 13: The Handmade House

p. 187 *"Who is this madwoman?"*: Linda Schierse Leonard, *Meeting the Madwoman: Empowering the Feminine Spirit* (Bantam, 1993), 3.

p. 189 *To* sacrifice *means "to make sacred"*: *Online Etymology Dictionary*, "sacrifice," last updated December 1, 2022, https://www.etymonline.com/word/sacrifice#etymonline_v_22581.

p. 189 *Once upon an autumn moon*: Based on "Rapunzel," collected by Jacob and Wilhelm Grimm, "Rapunzel," in *Kinder- und Hausmärchen gesammelt durch die Brüder Grimm*, 7th ed., trans D. L. Ashliman, vol. 1, no. 12 (Verlag der Dieterichschen Buchhandlung, 1857), 65–69, available at https://sites.pitt.edu/~dash/grimm012.html.

Conclusion

p. 201 *Once in a time long gone and still here*: Based on "The Sultan and His Vow," available at https://www.gutenberg.org/ebooks/19860.

p. 203 *Scheherazade means "noble lineage"*: Natasha Moura, "Who Was Scheherazade?," Womenart.com, August 12, 2020, https://womennart.com/2020/08/12/who-was-sheherazade/.

About the Author

Danielle Dulsky's work is rooted in wild spirituality, story, ritual, and humanity's deep, enduring, and embodied connection to the natural world. The founder of the Hag School and author of *Bones & Honey: A Heathen Prayer Book*; *The Holy Wild Grimoire: A Heathen Handbook of Magick, Spells, and Verses*; *Sacred Hags Oracle: Visionary Guidance for Dreamers, Witches, and Wild Hearts*; *Seasons of Moon & Flame: The Wild Dreamer's Epic Journey of Becoming*; *The Holy Wild: A Heathen Bible for the Untamed Woman*; and *Woman Most Wild: Three Keys to Liberating the Witch Within*, she holds a BA in painting from Arcadia University. A lover of Irish paganism, fiber art, old stories, and black cats, Danielle splits her time between the whiskey-soaked streets of a Pennsylvania steel town and the untamed grounds of upstate New York.

DanielleDulsky.com

TheHagSchool.com

Praise for *The Night House*

"In this enchanting book, Danielle Dulsky magickly re-visions many traditional fairy tales, reconnecting us to our wild, feral selves. Full of twists and surprises, this interactive and reflective book is masterfully written. *The Night House* forges a path to restore the natural order of our broken world."

— TRISTA HENDREN, author of *The Girl God*
and coeditor of *Re-Visioning Medusa*

"Danielle Dulsky not only invites us into mystical realms full of fairy tales and the magick and wisdom found within, but she builds a bridge from those tales into our own lives. She shows us how to travel the road of the imaginative seeker through the Night House and cross over the bridge with that magick intact, ready to transform our daily experiences of the mundane into endless meaning and connection, forever touched by the fleeting and mischievous creatures of myth. This is the kind of treasure-hunting symbolism and sensory-drenched storytelling that we need to awaken and integrate our most wild and loving selves."

— ORA NORTH, author of
I Don't Want to Be an Empath Anymore

"In *The Night House*, Danielle Dulsky gives us permission to embrace our personal paradox, the yearning for both stability and wildness, knowledge and innocence, solitude and connection. Her book provides support to walk our own path, guided by the lessons of light and shadow found in creative retellings of folk tales and myths from around the world. *The Night House* helps us weave our story and the world story together through ritual, altar work, journaling, and sacred practices, all the while humming our soul song, which we find with the support of the diverse cast of characters brought to vivid life through Dulsky's lyrical writing. Lovers of folk tales and myth will revel in this feast of stories that reveal, celebrate, and empower the wild nature within."

— CARMEN SPAGNOLA, author of
The Spirited Kitchen and *Spells for the Apocalypse*

Praise for *Bones and Honey* by Danielle Dulsky

"Danielle Dulsky artfully combines poetic allure with ancient insights, creating a narrative that profoundly touches the contemporary heart. Each page brims with nature-inspired prayers, mythic chants, and tales that rekindle our innate bond to the universe around us. Through her evocative prose, Danielle not only reshapes our understanding of prayer for today's world but also reignites the age-old connection between the reader and the natural realm. Her words stand as both a sanctuary and a revelation.... In a world on the edge, Danielle presents a haven of words and wisdom, a realm where souls can find comfort and inspiration."

— MAT AURYN, bestselling author of
Psychic Witch, Mastering Magick, and *Pisces Witch*

"The old ways of storytelling live on in these pages, offering medicine for wild hearts. Beautifully woven through prayers, spells, and stories, Danielle Dulsky's words speak straight to the beating heart of the human experience, in all its timeless expressions."

— CELESTE LARSEN, author of *Heal the Witch Wound*

"Danielle Dulsky is one of the most embodied truth sayers I have the pleasure of knowing."

— CHRIS GROSSO, author of
Indie Spiritualist and *Necessary Death*

THE
NIGHT
HOUSE

Also by Danielle Dulsky

Woman Most Wild: Three Keys to Liberating the Witch Within

The Holy Wild: A Heathen Bible for the Untamed Woman

Seasons of Moon and Flame:
The Wild Dreamer's Epic Journey of Becoming

Sacred Hags Oracle: Visionary Guidance for Dreamers, Witches,
and Wild Hearts (with illustrations by Janine Houseman)

The Holy Wild Grimoire:
A Heathen Handbook of Magick, Spells, and Verses

Bones & Honey: A Heathen Prayer Book